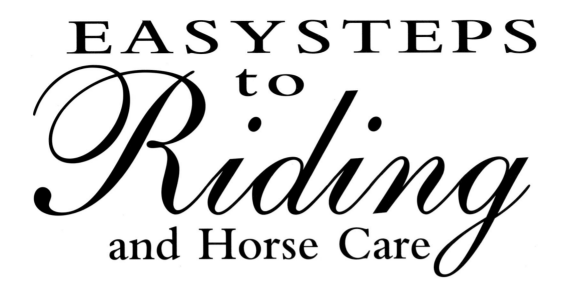

EASYSTEPS to Riding

and Horse Care

EASYSTEPS
to
Riding
and Horse Care

Nicole Smith

CHARTWELL
BOOKS, INC.

HW SC TH VWm

Published in 1996 by
Chartwell Books, Inc.
A division of Book Sales, Inc.
Raritan Center
114 Northfield Avenue
Edison, NJ 08818

Copyright © 1996
Regency House Publishing Limited

ISBN 0-7858-0601-6

Printed in Italy

THE PUBLISHERS WISH TO STRESS MOST EMPHATICALLY THAT PERSONS ENGAGING IN THE SPORT OF RIDING MUST NOT DO SO WITHOUT THE PROTECTION OF OFFICIALLY APPROVED HEADGEAR.

Photographic Acknowledgements

Brian Trodd: Pages 5, 6-7, 8, 9, 10, 11 bottom, 12, 13, 14-15, 16, 17, 18, 19, 20, 21, 24, 25, 29, 31 bottom, 32, 33, 34, 35, 37, 38, 39, 40, 45, 46, 47, 48 top left, bottom left, top right, 50, 52, 53, 54, 55, 56, 58, 59, 62, 63, 67, 72, 73, 74, 75, 76, 77.

Kit Houghton: Front cover, back cover, pages 2, 4, 11 top, 23, 26, 27, 28, 31 top, 36, 43, 44, 48 centre right, 49, 51, 57, 60, 61, 65, 66, 68, 69, 70, 71.

Regency House Publishing: Pages 10 top, 78, 79.

Annabel Trodd: Pages 41 42, 49 top left and right.

Linden Artists: Page 30.

The author would like to thank the following riders from Home Farm Stables: Zoe, Nicole, Lauren, and Charlotte. Many thanks also to Nicola and Hemsley Stables for their help with the photography and to the Shenley Stud for allowing us to photograph in their yard.

PAGES 2-3
Friends riding out in the countryside.

ABOVE
Pony Club Show Jumping.

RIGHT
A contented horse in his stable.

Contents

Introduction

This is a simple guide for young people who, while well aware of all the pitfalls, are more than eager to dedicate themselves wholeheartedly to the care of horses and the fascinating world of equestrianism.

Whether the young rider is using the facilities of the local riding school or is lucky enough to own his or her own horse or pony, it is essential to lay down good foundations in order to become a good rider later on.

Learning to halt, walk, trot and canter correctly will lead the rider on to the more fulfilling and exciting aspects of horsemanship. From riding for pleasure to the high-powered life of top competition, riding is a thoroughly absorbing and rewarding pastime.

It takes a good deal of time, patience and application to reach a good riding standard, but with determination and good schooling there is no reason why people of all ages and abilities cannot achieve a satisfactory level of competence.

It should never be forgotten, however, that, as with many other sports, there is an element of risk involved. You will notice, therefore, that the emphasis is concentrated on the safety of both horse and rider and the need to exercise absolute caution at all times.

Horses are complex and sensitive creatures, as easily upset by inappropriate feeding as they are by ill-fitting saddlery, both of which can make them uncomfortable, if not actually unwell. Even grooming, if carried out incorrectly, can be a potential hazard.

We must never lose sight of the fact that horses have their own strong likes and dislikes and each one has a distinct personality all its own.

Chapter One
Choosing the Right Horse for You

There exist so many excellent riding establishments these days that it is quite possible to hire a suitable horse as and when you require it. However, the rewards of building a life-long relationship with a pony of your own are undeniably great. Buying a horse or pony is not to be undertaken lightly; a weekly lesson at the local riding school is a far cry from being responsible for a horse of your own. First and foremost, it must be decided if the new pony is affordable. These days, a good one can cost a great deal of money and choosing one without expert advice is a daunting task. Once you have decided on the type of horse and the price you can afford, it will be necessary to inspect the local stables and livery yards to see how they are managed, what kinds of facilities they offer and what they cost.

Along with stabling, your new pony will require a whole range of tack, ranging from bridle and saddle,

BELOW
This 9-year-old Thoroughbred-type mare is in great condition and is an experienced all-rounder – the type of horse in which you could have a great deal of confidence.

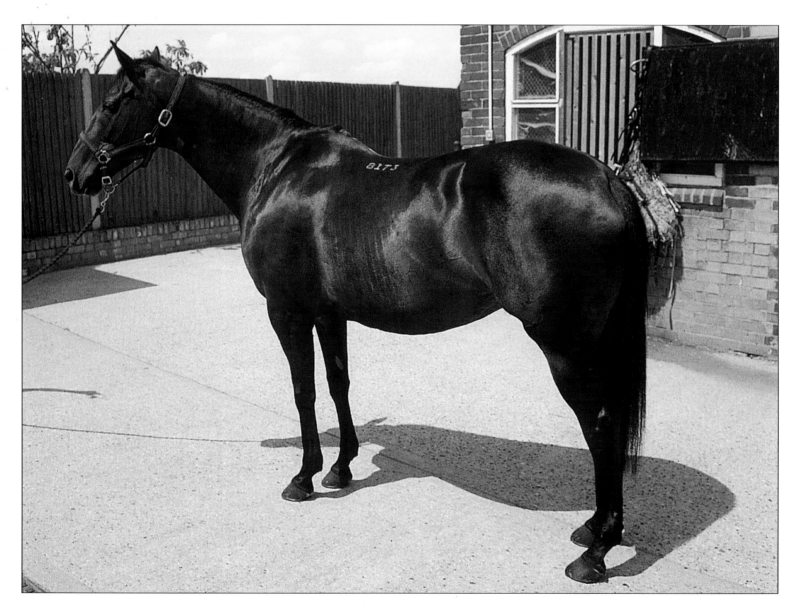

grooming kit, rugs and such items as haynets, buckets, etc. – all of which cost a lot of money. In addition to this, don't forget the range of equipment you will need for yourself.

Once you have decided that you can afford all this extra expense, you must be prepared to put in a lot of extra time. Horses and ponies need a great deal of attention; even horses at grass need to be visited daily to check their condition, feet and water supply.

It will not be necessary to ride your pony every day if he spends sufficient time in his field. Nevertheless, you must be prepared to devote more of your time at weekends and evenings unless help is at hand. Many riding schools offer a part-livery ser-

vice in exchange for which the school will use your pony for a proportion of the week when you are not riding him. This arrangement can be satisfactory from the financial point of view as well as providing your pony with regular exercise and extra help in grooming and mucking out.

Once you have a clear picture of the costs, the time involved and stabling requirements, the next stage is to look for your ideal pony.

It is virtually impossible to find a pony perfect in every respect and even if you could he would be beyond the means of the average person; therefore, we must look for a pony with as many good points as possible.

You can get to know when a good

Look for a pony with a kind, tranquil attitude. A pony who is happy and relaxed in the stable is likely to be easy to handle.

9

Points of the Horse

Poll

Crest

Ears

Mane

Forelock

Eye

Croup

Hindquarters

Withers

Nostril

Loins

Back

Cheek

Dock

Jugular Groove

Mouth

Tail

Chest

Shoulder

Sheath

Hock

Stifle

Chestnut

Knee

Cannon Bone

Fetlock

Pastern

Hoof

Coronet

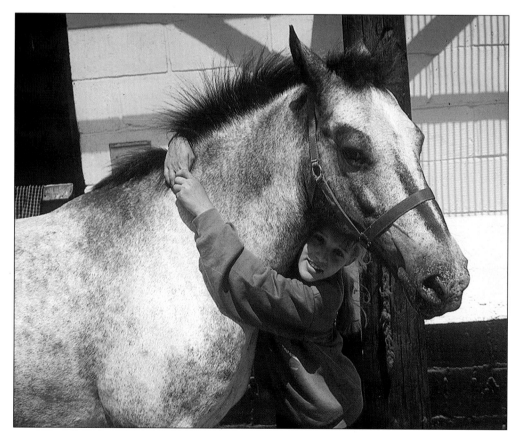

ABOVE
Get yourself acquainted with the points of the horse. It is helpful to know the correct terminology.

LEFT
It's great to find a pony who is also a good friend. This pony is quite happy to receive a hug from his owner.

horse is for sale by word of mouth or from friends, dealers or breeders; but whichever channel you choose, you should be very careful indeed. It is strongly recommended that you seek the advice and help of an experienced person who will be willing to accompany you in your search. The expertise of someone you trust can save an enormous amount of money and grief, as well as a wasted veterinary examination, which can be very expensive.

When you go to have a first look at a promising horse, take a look around the yard. See how the horses look in general. Do they look well cared for? How does the one you are interested in look in relation to the other horses in the yard? If he looks poor by comparison it could be that he is of unsound constitution which could cause problems in the future.

First, look at the new pony at rest in his stable. Is he friendly? Has he any vices e.g., weaving or windsucking – these are usually apparent while he is still in the stable. Pat him, talk to him and get to know him, but always remember that a strange horse is an unknown quantity.

The horse should be taken out

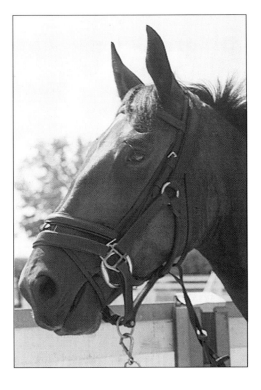

from his stable to enable you to take a good look at his conformation. At this stage, you should ask as many questions as possible and it is a good idea to have these questions ready and written down before your visit. This way, you will not leave the yard without asking questions that are vital. Some of the questions to ask are as follows: Is he thriving? Is he easy to catch? Is he amenable to boxing, shoeing, travelling? Does he have any allergies? How does he get along with the other horses in the field? Has he had any previous illnesses? Will he happily hack out alone and does he behave well in heavy traffic? – All of these questions are of primary importance. Of course the seller may not be

ABOVE
This young rider has found her ideal pony. Both are well suited to competitive riding and are thoroughly enjoying their day out.

LEFT
A bright, alert expression is very important when choosing a horse or pony. If he is happy and interested in his surroundings he is likely to be of a healthy and happy disposition.

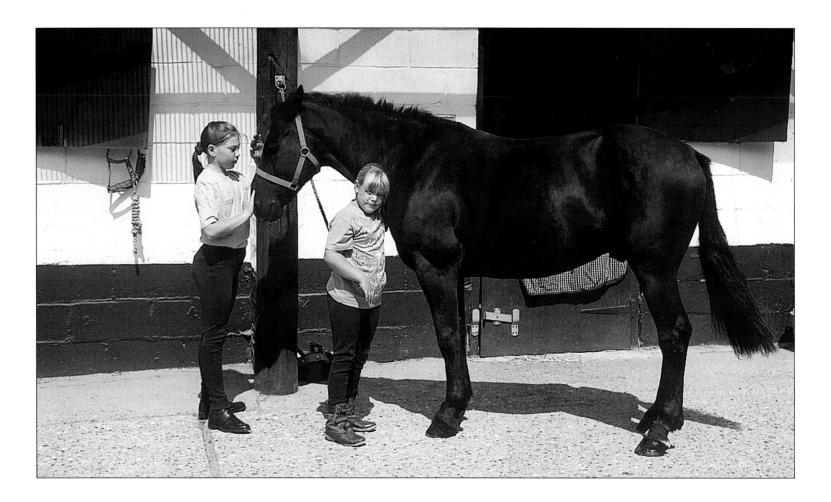

entirely truthful when replying to your questions; nevertheless, you should still be able to form a sound opinion with a little help from your knowledgeable friend.

Take the pony out of the stable so that he is standing on level ground while you have a close look at him. Is he well proportioned? Look at his head. The head should be the correct size for his body, his eyes should be kind and bright. His nostrils and ears should be clean and free from discharge. Go to the neck. The crest should be gently rounded with the neck neither too long or too short. A ewe neck is a sign of weakness and the horse should be avoided. Look at the legs. They should be straight, well proportioned and clean. Many blemishes, wind-galls, splints and spavins could well be a sign that he has done considerable work already and that his future mileage is limited. Look along the back. Is it nice and straight with plenty of room for the saddle. Look

for a horse with rounded, strong quarters and good sized hocks. It is advisable to get expert advice regarding conformation for it takes many years of experience to be able to spot serious defects. Ultimately, you are looking for an animal to do a job; the fact that he has weak hocks or hindquarters, while meaning that he is not good show jumper material, is unlikely to prevent him from being a perfectly good all-rounder; even being a little ugly and unlikely to star at shows will not necessarily prevent him from getting to the top in dressage! It is up to you, the purchaser, to decide for what purpose the horse is intended.

At this time, it is important to decide on an animal that is the right size for you. If you have not yet finished growing and are likely to get taller, it may be better to get a slightly larger pony than necessary. If other members of the family ride, it may be a good idea to look for an even larger animal still.

ABOVE
Get to know the pony you propose to buy. Pat him and handle him. Watch his reactions – a jumpy animal is likely to be nervous and unsuitable for an inexperienced rider.

RIGHT
This horse it contentedly watching the world go by. He is obviously calm and relaxed, a good start when looking at a prospective purchase.

What is he like to ride?

If you are satisfied so far, the next step is to tack up the pony and ride him. Is he easy to tack up? Hopefully, there will be somewhere safe to try him out. The best place is a manege or similar small fenced area. Ask the person selling the pony to ride him first. Notice how he goes in walk, trot and canter. Does he look sound? Is he well schooled? Make a note of anything you are unhappy about.

Now it's your turn to ride. Be extra careful with a strange horse. Do not take any chances. Ride him as you have been taught and be sympathetic with your aids so as not to alarm him. Remember, you are a stranger to him, too.

Once you are satisfied, you may like to progress a step further. The owner may let you take him out for a hack (do not go alone), or maybe let you try a jump or two.

In many cases, the owner may allow you to take the horse or pony for a trial period. This usually means that you will have a few weeks to get to know him and, in the event of finding him unsuitable can return him and get a full refund of money paid in advance. This is the best way to buy a pony and will enable you to make sure that you have come to the right decision.

Some horses, when sold, may come with a warranty guaranteeing their soundness. This is very reassuring for it means that were you to find anything physically wrong with him after getting him home, you would be entitled to your money back in full. An accompanying warranty is commonplace for horses sold at sales.

Once you are completely satisfied that this is the horse or pony for you, it is now time to find a suitable vet to come along and examine him. There are different degrees of vetting which come at varying degrees of cost. You can either opt for the most simple,

which will involve a thorough examination at the stable yard, or a more detailed vetting involving blood tests and X-rays.

Your vet will be very happy to explain his procedure to you in detail and will point out anything likely to affect the horse's health or future soundness. All this will help you to reach the ultimate decision – to buy, or not to buy.

At this stage, check if the horse has an up-to-date vaccination certificate. All horses and ponies should be vaccinated against flu and tetanus. If the horse in question is not covered, a new programme of vaccination should be commenced. This is particularly important for competition horses who are likely to travel regularly to different show grounds.

Once your pony passes the veterinary test and you have decided to proceed with the purchase, you are now faced with the job of getting him home. If you are lucky enough to own your own horsebox there is no problem; if not, you will have to hire one. Be cautious: hiring a horsebox for the day can be an expensive business, especially if the journey home is a long one. Check beforehand that the new pony is likely to load and travel satisfactorily. A difficult pony can take a long time to load onto a strange box. Make sure you have a full set of travelling gear as he must be fully protected while in transit.

LEFT
Trying out the pony you are interested in buying is very important. Always get the owner to try the pony first. This way you will see whether or not he is safe to ride.
Ride the pony for the first time in an enclosed space – a manege is most suitable.

15

Age

Age is an important issue to consider when buying a horse or pony. It may seem an attractive idea to buy a young horse, but in reality it can be a disastrous choice for the more inexperienced rider. Young horses are generally less predictable, naughtier, and more prone to developing bad habits; an older horse is likely be more dependable and safe: but there are no hard and fast rules. If you decide on an older horse you will have to accept that his working life will be more limited than that of a younger animal. An experienced person or vet will be able to determine the age of a pony by his teeth, although, as the pony becomes older, exact ageing becomes more difficult.

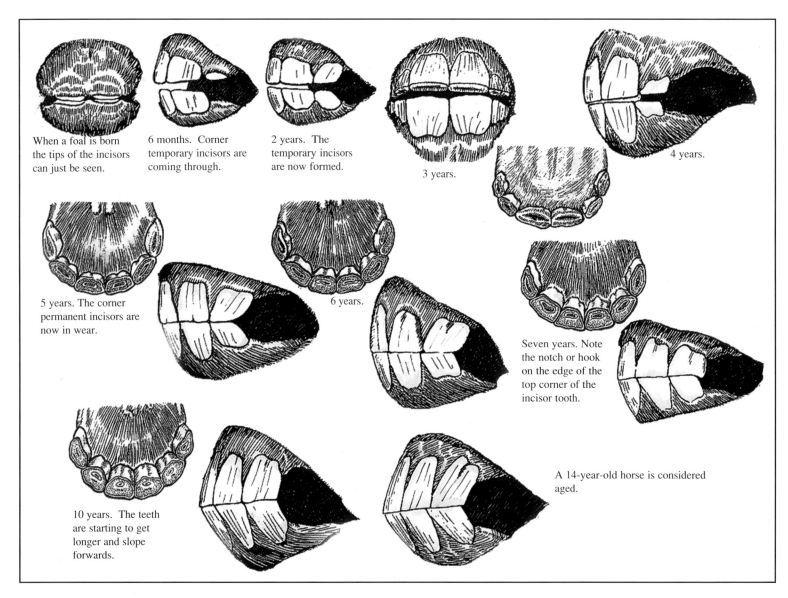

When a foal is born the tips of the incisors can just be seen.

6 months. Corner temporary incisors are coming through.

2 years. The temporary incisors are now formed.

3 years.

4 years.

5 years. The corner permanent incisors are now in wear.

6 years.

Seven years. Note the notch or hook on the edge of the top corner of the incisor tooth.

10 years. The teeth are starting to get longer and slope forwards.

A 14-year-old horse is considered aged.

Unsoundness

Generally speaking, we are looking for a horse sound in wind, eyes, heart and action – all of which are equally important. Your vet will be able to inform you about the first three, but you should be looking for potential sources of lameness on your first visit.

Find a hard, straight, level surface and have the horse walk up and down. Many potential causes of unsoundness are clearly visible from the walk. Next, he must be trotted up, his head allowed to swing freely. If you think he may be lame you should first decide which leg is involved – or maybe it is more than one. You must look for the seat of the lameness and finally the cause.

The following are some of the more common causes of lameness in horses.

Splint

A 'splint' is the name given to a bony enlargement that arises on the cannon and shannon bones. Splints can vary in size from a pea to a hen's egg. They can be caused by faulty conformation or repeated concussion. While a splint is forming, the horse will usually be lame, particularly at the trot.

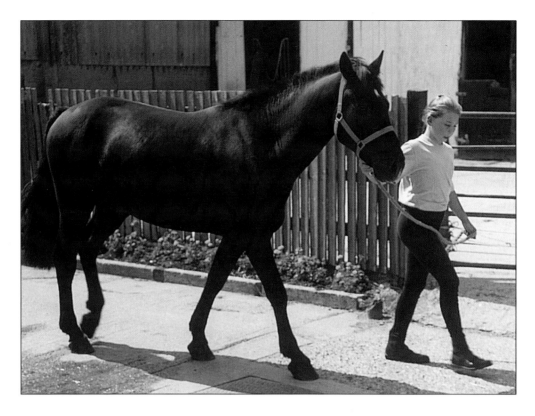

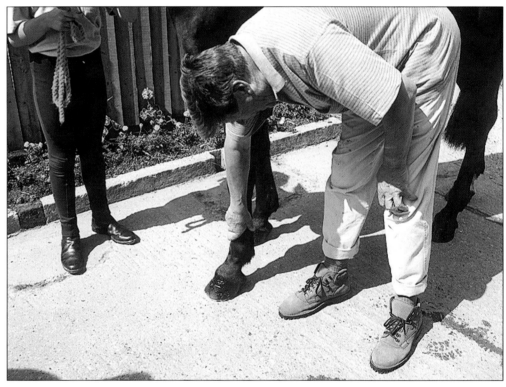

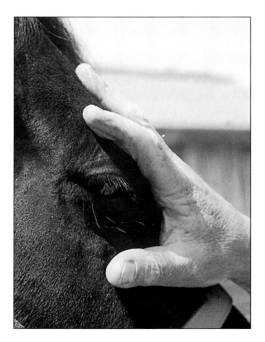

OPPOSITE ABOVE
A good look at your prospective pony's teeth will confirm his age. However, this inspection is best carried out by your vet.

OPPOSITE BELOW
Horses' teeth change as they get older: therefore their approximate age can be determined. This chart shows how a horse's teeth progress from newborn to 14 years of age when the teeth stop growing.

THIS PAGE
Before purchasing your pony, you must have him checked over by the vet for soundness of wind, eyes, heart and action.

17

Sprains

Muscles, tendons and ligaments are all affected by sprains. Sprains are generally caused by fast work, usually at gallop, and the symptoms are hotness and localized swelling.

Windgalls

Windgalls consist of soft swellings above the fetlock which are caused by wear or work but seldom cause lameness unless struck or knocked. Very few old horses are free of them.

Ringbone

Ringbone is a type of arthritis, located on the pastern, and can be caused by heavy work on hard ground. It is particularly common to the heavier breeds and can be hereditary. Ringbone does not usually cause lameness unless it occurs near a joint.

Corns

Corns in horses are very different from those in human beings. In the horse, it is a bruise between the wall of the hoof and the bar. Corns can produce varying degrees of lameness.

Navicular disease

Navicular disease is the best known cause of lameness and is found in the front and sometimes the back feet of all types of horses. The disease is caused by work on hard ground but can also be hereditary. Pain is inflicted by concussion of the coffin bone in the foot. The disease can be helped by corrective shoeing and drugs, but is generally considered incurable.

Bone Spavin

A bone spavin is a bony enlargement on the hock. It does not always cause lameness and many horses do recover completely.

Bog Spavin

The bog spavin is caused by strain and can cause severe lameness. The hock will be hot and inflamed. Rest and cold applications will help.

There are hundreds more diseases which can cause lameness and only your vet can really diagnose and treat them correctly. However, it is good to familiarize yourself with the more commonly found ailments.

Vices and Bad Habits

Weaving, wind-sucking, cribbing, kicking, attacking groom/shoe, bolting food, rug chewing – are all vices and habits which should be discouraged. Weaving causes wear to the forelimbs and cribbing damages the teeth. These kinds of bad habits are common, so it is wise to look out for them prior to making a purchase.

LEFT
Thorough inspection of the feet is essential.
RIGHT
This horse and rider are happy and contented with one other. They can look forward to a great relationship.

Chapter Two
Care – First Steps to Stable Management

The Stabled Horse

There are many advantages to keeping your pony stabled. He will be closer to hand and generally easier to groom and manage. However, a life spent in a stable is unnatural to him and compensations will have to be made. Feeding, grooming and exercise will have to mimic his natural way of life.

Feeding

The science of correct feeding is complex and there is a bewildering range of feeds from which to choose. There are some basic rules to follow and all of them are of equal importance.

Horses have small stomachs, in proportion to their size, and cannot cope very well with large meals. In their natural environment, they would be continuously grazing, consuming small amounts at a time. We must attempt to duplicate this in the domestic situation. Regular small feeds are therefore essential.

While your horse is in his stable he should have a continuous supply of water: if this is not possible, make sure he is given water before his feed. This will prevent the food from passing too quickly through the stomach.

A stabled horse needs plenty of bulk to chew on, such as hay. This again imitates natural conditions and keeps him happy and occupied.

It is essential that everything you feed your pony is of the best quality. Dusty or mouldy feed can be harmful and is a false economy. It is also a good idea to feed the stabled horse something succulent every day. Carrots are the ideal food and a favourite of all horses and ponies,

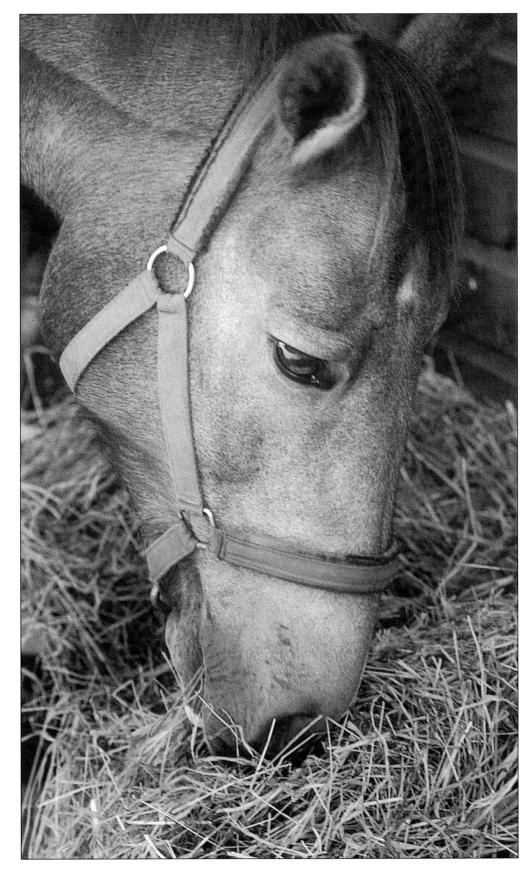

LEFT
A stabled pony eating hay. It is important to follow a strict feeding régime which should be an imitation of the pony's natural feeding habits. When he is feeding, make sure he has plenty of peace and quiet.

ABOVE
There are many different kinds of feeds to choose from but it is important to seek expert advice when putting together your pony's feeding timetable.

helping to replace fresh grass in their diet.

Do not take your pony out for a vigorous ride after a feed or when his stomach is very full of grass. Allow the food to go down for at least an hour before exercise.

Horses should be regularly wormed and there are a variety of excellent preparations available for this purpose. Instructions for using them should be carefully followed in every detail. It is also recommended that different brands are used in rotation to prevent tolerance to one particular product developing. Usually, you should treat your horse or pony every six weeks or so. The wormer may be added in pow-

der form to the horse's shortfeed or syringed directly into his mouth.

The amount of feed a horse requires depends upon the amount of exercise he gets as well as his temperament. A hunter or event horse needs rather more food than a small pony exercised mainly at weekends. In fact, all heating foods, e.g. oats, should not be fed to ponies without expert advice.

There are many complete feeds to choose from as well as special manufactured feeds for mares and foals, small ponies, competition horses and race horses. These feeds contain many of the basic elements listed as follows:-

Oats: Oats are high in protein and provide a great deal of energy. They are usually fed crushed. Generally, they should be used for horses who are in heavy or fast work. They must only be fed in accordance with the amount of exercise the horse gets.

Sugar Beet: This is fed well soaked and is used primarily for giving bulk to the feed.

Maize: Maize is fed flaked to provide energy and vitamins.

Barley: This is usually fed crushed and is fattening. It should not be fed to competition horses.

Bran: Bran is a good source of bulk and has good laxative properties. For ill or tired horses, a bran mash is easy to digest and will help recovery.

Linseed: Boiled and mixed with feed, linseed helps encourage a glossy coat.

Horse Nuts: Nuts come in many forms and you can choose the correct one for your horse or pony. Make sure plenty of fresh water accompanies this form of feed.

Mixes: Mixes can be given as a complete food together with hay. There are many different kinds, catering for different types of horses.

Hay: For the stabled horse, hay makes up the bulk of his feed. Always buy the best quality available. Dusty hay can cause respiratory diseases.

Chaff: Is chopped hay and a good source of bulk. It also slows down eating, thus aiding digestion.

Note: Horses who are regularly turned out in a good field with high quality grass may need slightly less supplementary feeding. However, a careful eye should be kept on them to monitor weight gain or loss and their general condition checked. It must be remembered that deciding the correct type of feeding takes experience and advice should always be sought before commencing a feeding routine.

FEEDING SUGGESTIONS

Based on the horse or pony stabled at night and turned out for a period during the day with access to good grazing

	7.30am	Midday	5.00pm	7.30pm
13.2hh pony, lightly worked	450g (1lb) pony mix 450g (1lb) sugar beet 450g (1lb) pony nuts		450g (1lb) pony mix 450g (1lb) sugar beet 450g (1lb) pony nuts	4.5kg (10lb) hay net
14.2hh pony, lightly ridden	900g (2lb) pony mix 450g (1lb) sugar beet 450g (1lb) pony nuts		450g (1lb) pony mix 450g (1lb) sugar beet 450g (1lb) pony nuts	5.5kg (12lb) hay net
14.2hh pony, regular work	900g (2lb) pony mix 450g (1lb) sugar beet 450g (1lb) pony nuts 450g (1lb) oats		900g (2lb) pony mix 450g (1lb) sugar beet 450g (1lb) pony nuts	5.5kg (12lb) hay net
15.2hh horse, lightly ridden	900g (2lb) horse mix 450g (1lb) sugar beet 450g (1lb) nuts		900g (2lb) horse mix 450g (1lb) sugar beet 450g (1lb) nuts	5.5kg (12lb) hay net
15.2hh horse, in hard work	900g (2lb) competition mix 450g (1lb) sugar beet 450g (1lb) oats 3.6 kg (8lb) hay net	900g (2lb) competition mix 450g (1lb) sugar beet 450g (1lb) oats	900g (2lb) competition mix 450g (1lb) sugar beet 450g (1lb) oats	5.5kg (12lb) hay net
16.2hh horse, in hard regular work	900g (2lb) competition mix 450g (1lb) sugar beet 450g (1lb) oats 3.6 kg (8lb) hay net	900g (2lb) competition mix 450g (1lb) sugar beet 450g (1lb) oats	900g (2lb) competition mix 450g (1lb) sugar beet 450g (1lb) oats	5.5kg (12lb) hay net 450g (1lb) oats 450g (1lb) sugar beet

ABOVE
This pony is in fine condition. His carefully balanced feeding programme, combined with
regular exercise and careful grooming, is bound to ensure his success in the show ring.

Mucking Out

Stabled horses should be thoroughly mucked out every day to ensure that they remain happy and healthy. There are many different types of bedding to chose from. Straw is the most common and is comfortable and cosy. Wheat makes the best kind of straw and is the most easily obtainable. Barley and oat straw are other suitable options. However, both are so palatable that you may turn up to muck out in the morning only to find that your pony has eaten his bed!

Horses who are allergic to straw, prone to eating their beds, or are very messy, are better kept on wood shavings. These make an excellent bed being both comfortable and soft. The main drawback is that they are rather expensive.

Rubber matting and shredded paper are becoming increasingly popular. Both save money and are good alternatives to the traditional beddings.

The main tool for mucking out is the fork. The modern lightweight forks are best and help to make the

job easier. You will also need a good wheelbarrow, a shovel and a broom. A rake is good for a shavings bed.

Step 1.

First, remove all water buckets, feed bowls and hay nets from the stable. These things, if left inside, will get in the way and hamper your progress. You *can* muck out with your pony tied up in the stable. However, if you have somewhere to put him outside, your job will be a lot easier.

Remove the heavily soiled matter straight into the wheelbarrow. Then sort out the clean straw from the dirty. Sift through it carefully and try not to waste good straw. It is best to put all the clean straw in one corner, then you can give the floor a good sweep.

TIP *It's a good idea to pick out your pony's feet before you muck out. This will save time later.*

Step 2.
All the remaining straw in the stable can be forked into the centre leaving slightly less at the edges. Make sure the bed is carefully flattened to prevent the horse from kicking it up too much.

Step 3.
Collect some clean straw. You will soon get to know how much you will need to replenish the bed. Start off by forking up clean straw around the edges of the bed to make banks. This will make your horse more comfortable and help prevent injury. Then put clean straw over the whole bed. Check that the bed is deep and flat. It is not recommended that you shake up the clean straw while your horse is in the stable as the dust will be thrown up into his face.

Step 4.
Go to the manure pile and empty your wheelbarrow. Make sure the muck is thrown to the top of the pile. Now put your tools tidily away.

Step 5.
Give the water buckets a good scrub and fill them up with clean water.

In fine weather, you may wish to clean your stable out completely and disinfect it. Make sure you allow plenty of time for the stable to dry out before putting fresh bedding down.

For permanently stabled horses, it is a good idea to skip out a few times during the day or whenever droppings appear. This will help prevent odour and keep the bed cleaner in the long run.

More bedding can be added later to ensure a good night's sleep. Make sure your pony has enough water to last the night and be sure to turn all the lights off.

ABOVE AND LEFT
Mucking out is hard work, though satisfying. The daily routine is a rewarding part of stable management. A good set of the correct tools for the job is a sound investment and will help you achieve a better end result. Whether on wood chip, straw or shredded paper, your pony will really appreciate a good, clean, deep bed.

Keeping Your Pony at Grass

This should never be considered a cheap or easy option for, in many ways, grass-kept horses need even more careful monitoring. Good grazing is always difficult to find and there are many factors to be considered before deciding on this course of action.

Fencing: One of the most important priorities is a good safe fence. Every year, many horses are injured in dangerously fenced fields and many veterinary surgeons will tell you that the amount of time attending to injuries caused by barbed wire takes up a huge percentage of their time. The most preferred type of fencing is post and rail. Post and wire is another good option, but the strands need to be well maintained and kept tightly stretched. A dense hedge is a safe and natural barrier as are dry stone walls. In every case, regular checks and maintenance should be carried out and holes immediately mended as they appear. Barbed wire is definitely not recommended anywhere near horses, for obvious reasons. A good gate is vital and there are many excellent examples to choose from such as the traditional wooden five-bar gate or even a well designed metal one. Last but not least, always close the gate behind you and padlock it if you are going to leave horses out at night.

Grazing: The quality of grazing land is most important and the amount of land required per horse will vary depending on the quality of the land. Generally speaking, a horse requires at least 0.8 hectares (2 acres) of grass to sustain him for six months. Fields should be regularly rested and allowed to recover. In springtime there may be too much grazing; if necessary, the field can be sectioned off with electric fencing to prevent the horses from eating too much. At this time of year horses, and particularly ponies who are susceptible to laminitis, should be kept away from large areas of rich grass.

Overgrazed fields soon become weedridden and infested with worms. Grazing land should be regularly inspected for debris and dangerous items. It is also a good idea to pick up droppings as they accumulate. This keeps down the worm population and encourages the grass to stay in good condition. Raking or harrowing is also beneficial for grazing land.

It is not recommended that Thoroughbred-type horses are left to winter out and in Canada and parts of the United States it may not be practical or kind to leave a pony out all winter when temperatures fall to extremely low values.

BELOW
This is a good example of a type of fencing safe for horses. Post and rail is the best kind, though very expensive.

RIGHT
This horse is happy and content in his summer field. Do not allow horses to become too overweight in the spring and summer months.

Water Supply: It is absolutely necessary to have a good, fresh water supply in your field. Horses drink a far greater amount of water than most people suppose. On a hot summer's day, dehydration can rapidly set in if your pony does not have access to a constant supply. A self-filling water trough with a ballcock mechanism is the best option. Remember to scrub out the trough regularly with clean water to avoid the build-up of algae. In very cold weather you must remember to break the ice on the top of the trough to allow the horses to drink.

Shelter: Horses and ponies kept out at grass all year round need protection. Ideally, the best kind of shelter is a three-sided wooden or brick structure with a south-facing entrance. If the shelter is protected by trees and hedges, so much the better. If possible, the floor should be of concrete and extend to the area outside the shelter to prevent the ground from

becoming poached. Your horse will also be able to use his shelter in the heat of summer to escape from irritating flies. If it is impossible to provide a sturdy shelter, at least make sure the field has plenty of natural protection such as high, thick hedges and plenty of trees. This will provide at least some degree of shelter from sun and cold winds. Under no circumstance should you expect your horse to live in a field without shelter of any kind.

A good New Zealand rug will help to see your pony through the winter and if it is very cold you could put another well fitting rug underneath it.

Last but not least, horses wintering out must have food. There is little nourishment in grass during the winter months and you will need to supplement their diet with a liberal supply of hay and an adequate amount of shortfeed. Once the spring and summer months arrive, the amount of supplementary foods can be reduced.

LEFT
British native breeds are tolerant to severe conditions in the winter months. However, good shelter and adequate feeding are essential for health and fitness.

ABOVE
Whatever the weather, horses love to roll. Cleaning off muddy horses can prove a long and arduous task. It is essential that all mud is removed, particularly from the legs and belly.

Poisonous plants

Noxious weeds proliferate in every field. They should be promptly recognized, dug up and destroyed. Yew and laburnum are probably the most deadly, but hemlock, ragwort, privet, foxglove and laurel are also very poisonous.

General distress and discomfort can often be a sign of poisoning. The horse may show signs of stomach pain and saliva will begin to flow freely from his mouth. Take the animal into his stable and call for the vet as a matter of urgency. Have a good look round the field and see if you can identify what he may have eaten. This may well be of help to the vet when it comes to prescribing treatment.

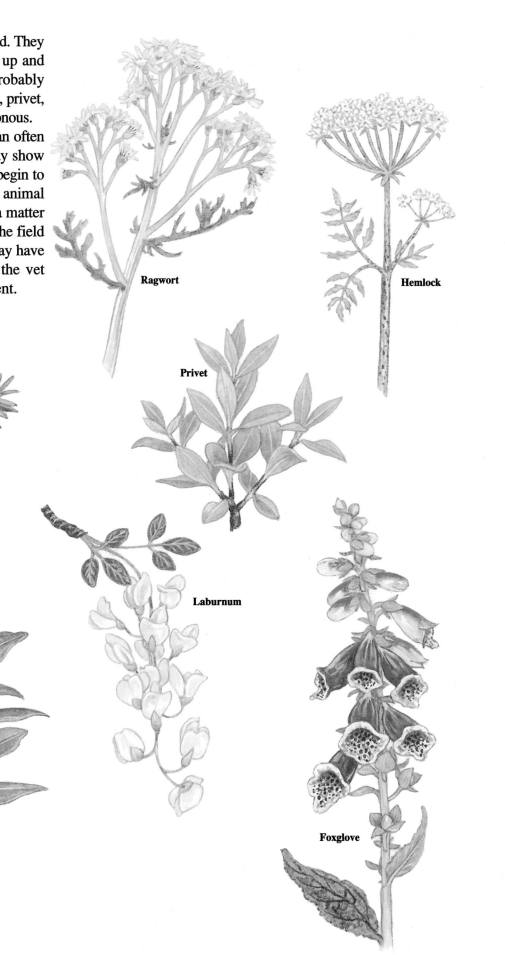

Ragwort

Hemlock

Privet

Yew

Laburnum

Laurel

Foxglove

Catching Your Pony: Take the head collar and leading rope with you into the field. Hold the head collar low and still against your side when approaching the horse. Approach him from the side, steadily. If he proves difficult to catch, tempt him with some horse nuts or a carrot or two. When you have him eating from your hand, put his head collar on gently. To catch a very stubborn pony, you may need to take a bucket with a few nuts in it. Once caught, lead your pony to a dry, level place where you can tie him up.

Daily Routine: First, check over your pony for injuries. Next, check his feet. Pick them all out with a hoof pick and scrub them out with a stiff brush. Once a week, it is a good idea to give the feet a good scrub with clean water both inside and out. This will help keep them free from bacteria and prevent infection occurring.

Next, give your pony a grooming to remove all the mud from his coat. For ponies at grass it is not necessary to do a thorough grooming with a fine body brush – you do not wish to remove vital oils from the coat which help keep it waterproof. Finally, tackle the mane and tail with a soft brush or comb. Once you are satisfied that all is clean and tidy, the pony can be exercised, fed, and left in the field. Horses and ponies are social animals and are generally happier in the company of others. If possible, try to avoid leaving your pony alone in his field.

The Combined System

Most people prefer to combine a partly stabled and partly grazed régime for their pony. The best system in winter is to leave the horse in his stable at night and put him out during the day. This means that he avoids the harshest weather but can roam and graze in the warmer daylight hours. In summer, many people prefer to keep their pony in his stable during the day

where he can shelter from heat and flies and at night graze happily in the field. Keeping him in a stable during the day also cuts down the amount of grass he eats which is important for weight control. This system ensures that your pony can be more easily exercised and managed but at the same time enjoy the benefits of a natural life.

All ponies at grass should be visited twice a day.

Security

Nowadays, the modern stable yard is home to an array of very expensive equipment, not forgetting the horses and ponies themselves, so there is a great need for good security. Most tack rooms need to be alarmed as well as locked and windows should be barred.

Freeze branding is one of the best ways of preventing horses from being stolen. The horse's skin is humanely marked by freeze branding it with his identifying details. These details are

then entered in a national register together with the owner's name. Should the horse be stolen, the true owner can be immediately identified and his property hopefully restored to him.

TOP
When catching your pony, remember to approach him quietly from the side, keeping the head collar low and still. A few carrots will act as a good incentive.

ABOVE
A good example of freeze branding.

LEFT
Illustrated here are just a few of the most poisonous plants. There are many more all of which the horse owner should be able to identify.

Chapter Three
Rugs and Blankets

There are many different types of rugs available and making the right choice can be a bewildering task.

New Zealand Rug: This is traditionally made of green canvas. Nowadays, however, a variety of man-made materials are also used, making them just as hardwearing and waterproof. Ideally, New Zealands are lined with wool for extra warmth but, again, synthetic fabrics are just as often used. This type of rug is for horses at grass in bad weather where it will greatly protect them from the harsher elements, particularly rain. It will be subjected to a great deal of wear and tear and will need to be serviced, repaired and regularly re-proofed. The best New Zealands have leg straps which should be looped through each other between the horse's back legs. Cross-over straps, which go underneath the horse's belly, also prevent the rug from slipping. Some very well tailored rugs do not need cross-over straps and are self-righting.

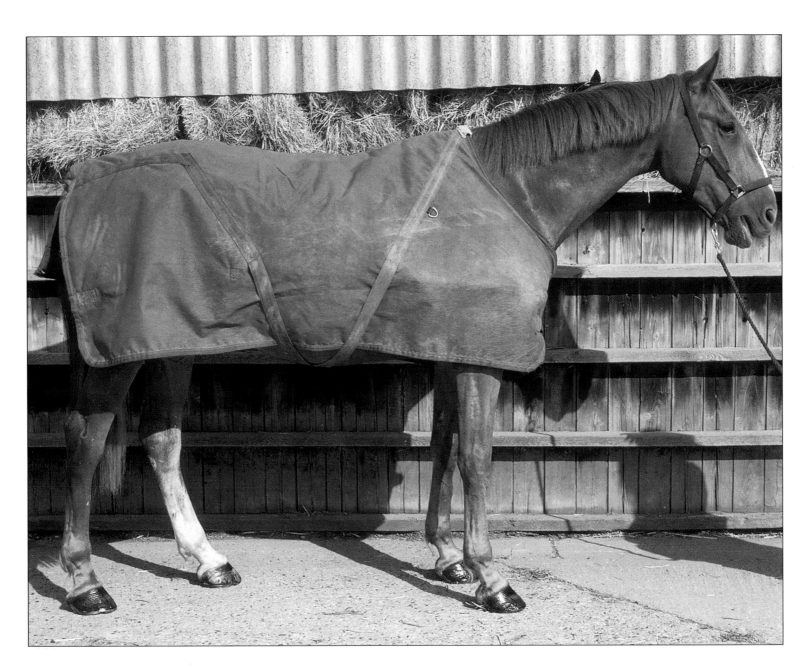

FAR LEFT
This modern-style New Zealand rug is hardwearing, waterproof and rip proof. Correctly serviced and maintained, it will give many years of protection. The more traditional New Zealand is made from green canvas lined with wool. All New Zealands come with various leg straps and surcingles which must be correctly fitted to ensure safety.

LEFT
Some ponies love to roll and many feel the cold. This neck cover will keep them clean and warm. Modern stable and New Zealand rugs come with attachments to which a neck cover can be fitted, which can be bought separately.

BELOW
This quilted nylon stable rug is easily washed in the washing machine and is lightweight and smart. There are a wide variety of stable rugs to choose from ranging from the ones manufactured from simple jute to more luxurious and expensive fabrics such as wool.

Stable Rug: The stable rug is designed for horses and ponies who are kept in. There are many different kinds to choose from. The nylon quilted rug with a cotton lining is the most popular and has the added advantage of being easy to wash in a washing machine. It is lightweight and comfortable and more than one can be piled on in cold weather for extra warmth.

The wool stable rug is also popular. It comes in many different colours and can also be striped. It is extremely warm and great for horses who are clipped out in the winter. It can be used underneath a nylon rug to provide even greater warmth. One drawback is that it is more difficult to wash and liable to shrinkage. Bedding can also get caught up in the weave and be difficult to remove.

The jute stable rug is a rather more traditional type. Good value and very warm, it should be worn with a roller to prevent slippage.

Summer Sheet: The summer sheet is manufactured from light cotton, usually with cross-over straps and a fillet string. It comes in a variety of colours and is easy to wash and maintain.

The rug is useful in hot weather for protecting your pony from flies when he is out in the field. It can also be used to keep dust out of his coat when travelling. Show competitors sometimes use the summer sheet to throw over their pony to keep him clean and tidy while he is waiting his turn.

Sweat Sheet: The sweat sheet is a loosely woven cotton rug, rather like a string vest, and comes in many different colours. It is used when horses have been sweating profusely and need to cool off slowly. It should be used with another rug on top. Air is trapped in the pockets of the weave which helps the animal to dry off, preventing him from cooling down too rapidly and becoming chilled.

Underblanket: An underblanket can be used under any rug for extra warmth, but must be carefully folded and fitted to prevent it from slipping.

This is an inexpensive option for the price-conscious horse owner.

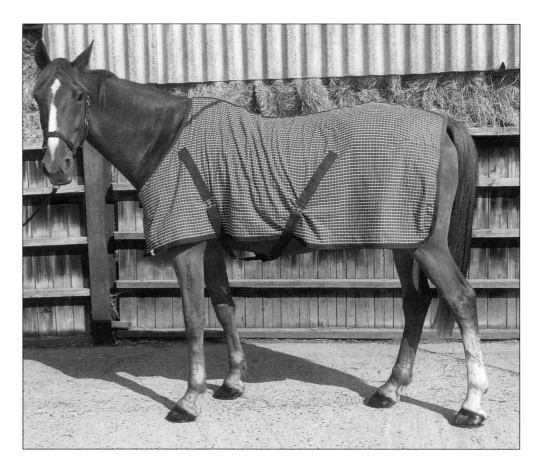

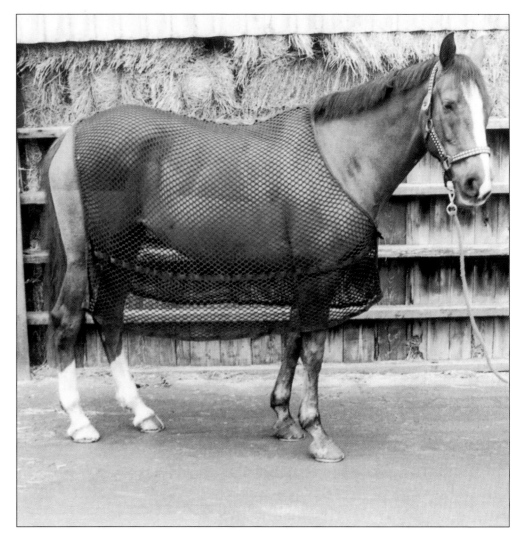

LEFT
The gold, red and black-striped English Witney stable rug will make any horse look smart and handsome at the show or keep him comfortable in his stable. Natural wool is still one of the finest materials available, keeping the horse warm and snug and the skin still able to breathe.

TOP RIGHT
A traditional summer sheet with cross-over straps.

RIGHT
A smart sweat sheet is a vital piece of equipment for all horse owners.

Chapter Four
Grooming – The Daily Routine

ABOVE
The daily routine of grooming helps to keep this horse's coat in tip-top condition.

ABOVE RIGHT
The basic items in a grooming kit are illustrated here. Keep your kit tidy and in good order and it will give you many years of service.

CENTRE RIGHT
Picking out the feet daily is one of the most important aspects of the grooming routine. Early detection of foot problems can help prevent possible future lameness.

RIGHT
The dandy brush is a hard brush useful for removing mud.

Grooming your pony is a vital part of his maintenance and he is likely to enjoy it as well. There are a number of tools you will need to buy, nearly all of which are necessary. Regular grooming will add to his health and well-being. Depending on your own level of expertise, you should spend about half an hour a day on the task. While grooming, remember that your pony is quite capable of giving you a nip out of boredom or mischief, so always be alert to the fact. Remember also never to stand directly behind him – he could well suddenly decide to kick out. Always pass around his front end

and make this a regular habit.

Commence by picking out each foot with a hoof pick. Make sure that the insides of the feet are free from mud and, if they are very dirty, scrub them out with a water brush. Pick out the feet in a downward motion to avoid damaging the sensitive frog. At the same time, it is a good idea to check the state of the shoes. Are they still firm and tight? Make sure the nails have not worked loose and there are no rough edges. Early detection of a loose shoe will give you plenty of time to make an appointment with the farrier before the shoe is cast and damage to the foot is caused.

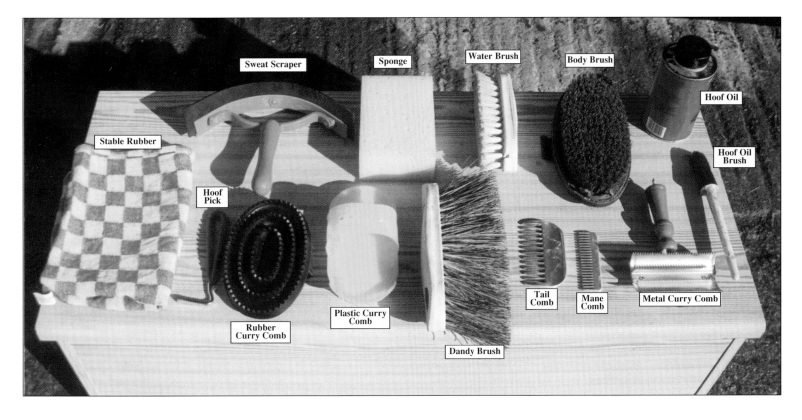

Sweat Scraper · Sponge · Water Brush · Body Brush · Hoof Oil · Hoof Oil Brush · Stable Rubber · Hoof Pick · Rubber Curry Comb · Plastic Curry Comb · Dandy Brush · Tail Comb · Mane Comb · Metal Curry Comb

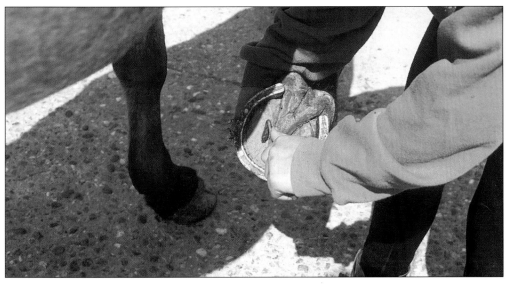

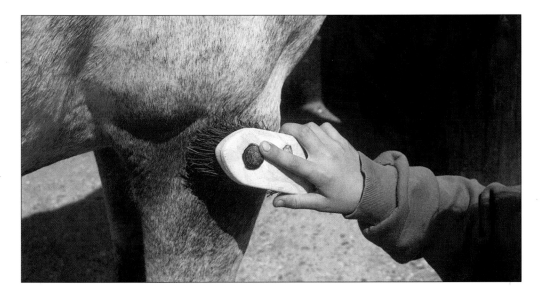

The next stage is to use the dandy brush to remove all mud from the coat. This brush is very hard and care should be taken not to scratch any sensitive areas. If your pony has a long coat he is unlikely to be bothered by its harshness; but if he is clipped, or a Thoroughbred-type, extra care should be taken. Do not use this brush on the head.

Once spring comes, a rubber curry comb is essential for removing excess hair from the horse's coat. Horses moult constantly for about 6 weeks providing plenty of work for you to do.

The next stage of grooming is the mane and tail. Start with a soft body brush and remove all tangles, mud and dust. You can finish off with a comb, but make sure all tangles have first been removed. Small amounts of untidy hair can be pulled from mane and tail to keep them neat, but beware, practice is needed to perfect this technique. Generally speaking, a horse's tail should hang about 3 inches below the hock and a regular trim with scissors will keep it neat. The mane should lie neatly on the off side

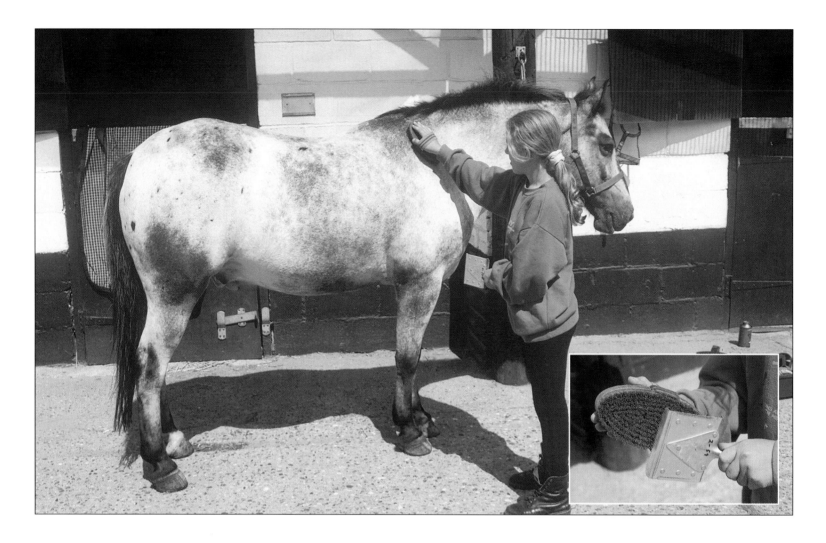

neck and the mane should be kept short enough to be tidy but long enough to plait, when necessary. In summer, when the weather is hot and the pony is badly irritated by flies, you may wish to leave the mane and forelock a little longer in length to give added protection to the eyes.

Now that the worst of the dirt has been removed, it is time for the finishing touches. The body brush is made from soft fibres and is used to remove fine dust and grease from the coat. It is essential that after each stroke the brush is cleaned with a metal curry comb. This implement is strictly for cleaning out brushes and must not be used on a horse's coat. A stable rubber, which is really a cotton cloth, can be used for a final polish.

Water brushes and sponges can be used for washing very dirty areas. A separate clean sponge should be used for cleaning the nostrils and around

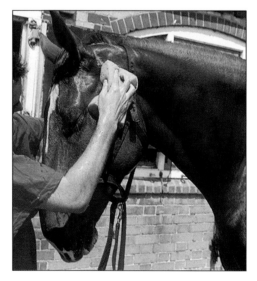

the eyes and kept specifically for the purpose. On hot days, or in preparation for a special show or event, it may be necessary to give your pony a good all-over wash. Use a special horse shampoo – this can be bought from any saddlery shop – following the instructions on the bottle carefully. Some horse shampoos contain fly

ABOVE AND INSET
The body brush is soft and is used to remove dirt and dust from the coat. After each stroke, clean the brush out with a metal curry comb.

LEFT
On a hot day, especially after exercise, your horse will really appreciate a wipe with a wet sponge around the face and eyes. Keep a sponge specifically for this purpose.

ABOVE RIGHT
Brush the tail regularly with a soft brush. This will keep it shiny and tangle free.

RIGHT
Before the show, or on a very hot day, it may be necessary to give your pony an all-over wash. Use a special horse shampoo and remember to rinse off very well as excess shampoo left on the skin could cause irritation. Dry him off with a clean towel and walk him around in the sunshine. Make sure he does not get cold.

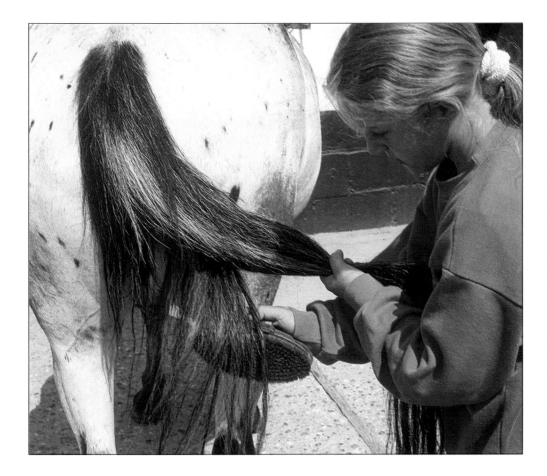

repellents which provide some comfort for ponies left out in the field during the summer months. After you have shampooed your pony, rinse his coat very thoroughly, then use a sweat scraper to remove all the surplus water from his coat. A good rub-down with a clean towel is now appropriate, the mane and tail being thoroughly groomed and a bandage applied to the tail. This will give a better finish and the hair will lie tidily when it is dry. If it is a nice day, take him for a walk in the sunshine to dry off. This way, drying is hastened and he will be less likely to catch cold. A sweat rug would also be useful for this purpose. For improved muscle tone, a hay wisp can be used. Slap the coat, in the same direction as the lie of the hair, with a bunch of damp hay. Your horse should really enjoy this procedure which is best done directly after exercise.

Chapter Five
Clipping, Shoeing, First Aid & Dental Care

The aim of clipping is to aid the comfort and performance of the horse in winter. Once summer is over, all horses start to grow a winter coat which varies in thickness and quality depending upon the breed. At this time of year, you will find that even the lightest exercise will cause your horse to sweat profusely and as the weather becomes progressively colder and the coat heavier, fast work will become more difficult and distressing for him. This is an indication that it is time for a clip. Horses and ponies should be clipped only if they are stabled at night in winter although it is fine to turn them out during the day protected by a good New Zealand rug. If you plan to winter your horse completely at grass it is unfair to clip him as he will need all his natural protection. There are many different clips and you should choose one appropriate to the type of work your pony does and his type of coat – if he has a heavy natural coat and you are planning very fast work, such as eventing or hunting, you will need a fuller clip. A clipped horse is easier to groom and dry off. This is of great benefit to both horse and owner during the winter months.

Trace Clip: This is where only the minimum amount of hair is removed. It is suitable for horses and ponies engaged in moderate work who will benefit from having some hair removed from the neck and other areas prone to sweating. This is a good clip for horses who are turned out during the day as many of the most exposed areas remain unclipped.

Blanket Clip: This takes the trace clip a stage further. The hair is entirely removed from the neck, keeping the horse that little bit cooler than if he only had a trace clip.

Hunter Clip: This removes all the hair from the horse's body except for the legs and saddle area. It is only suitable for stabled horses who are regularly hunted or evented.

Whichever clip you choose, you must compensate for what you have removed by rugging the horse up to give him the necessary protection. In especially cold weather, the number of rugs should be increased and in warm spells reduced; but whatever the case, careful monitoring and attention are required.

Clipped horses should not be turned out into a field without a New Zealand rug and in more severe weather an under rug will also be required. It is essential that a clipped horse is kept extra clean and free from mud as his skin has lost the natural protection of its own very thick coat.

In prolonged or very wet weather you should beware of mud fever which is brought on by the cold and wet.

LEFT
This horse has been given a blanket clip. Throughout the winter period, he must be regularly tidied up with horse clippers to ensure he stays smart all season.

RIGHT
The three main styles of clip are illustrated here. From the trace to the full hunter clip, each one is designed to suit the individual horse's work load.

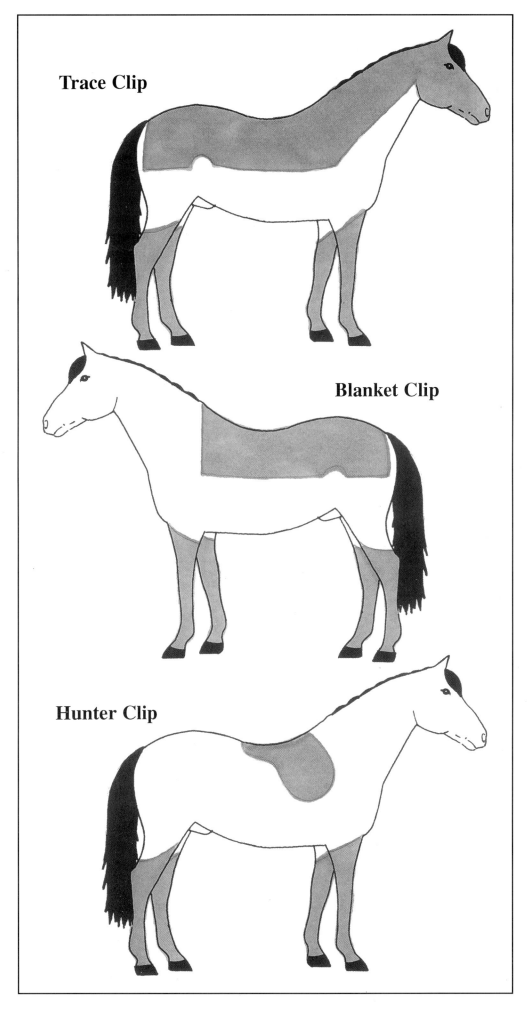

Trace Clip

Blanket Clip

Hunter Clip

Shoeing

Regular shoeing will keep your horse's feet in good condition and help prevent many of the diseases which could ultimately lead to lameness. The lifestyle of the horse has undergone tremendous changes since his days of roaming free. Man-made roads, the added weight of a rider and the many other demands we make of him mean that for all his working life he will have to wear metal shoes on his feet. Shoeing is a highly skilled operation which should only be undertaken by a qualified farrier. You are likely to need a visit from your farrier every 4 to 6 weeks, depending upon your horse's requirements. The farrier will tell you what type of shoes are appropriate and will be happy to advise on any problems concerning the health of your horse's feet.

There are two different types of shoeing to choose from – 'hot' and 'cold'. Hot shoeing is far superior because the shoe can be made to a better fit. This is because metal, when heated, becomes more pliable and the farrier will find it easier to work. In cold shoeing, it is more difficult to fit the shoe to the foot, although it is considered the best option for horses who are either fearful of the farrier or have very weak feet.

The farrier will first remove the old shoes. He will then cut away any excess growth of horn, rasping the surface of the foot. Next, he will fit the new shoes onto the foot. This can be done either hot or cold. After making the necessary adjustments, the farrier will nail the shoe to the hoof, usually with three nails on the inside and four on the outside. The heads of the nails are hammered down and flattened. Finally, the heads are rasped to give a smooth finish.

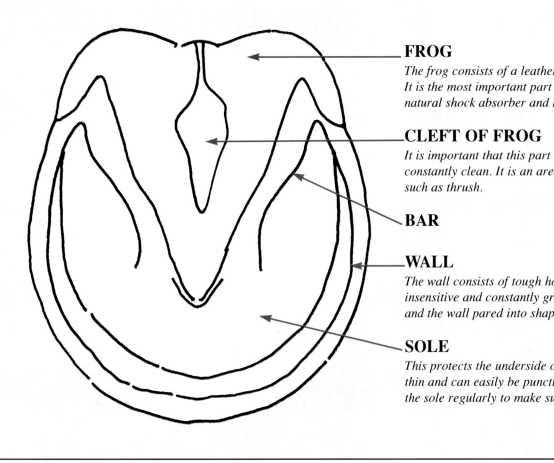

FROG

The frog consists of a leathery substance and is 'V-shaped'. It is the most important part of the hoof, providing a natural shock absorber and non-slip pad.

CLEFT OF FROG

It is important that this part of the foot is kept constantly clean. It is an area which is prone to disease such as thrush.

BAR

WALL

The wall consists of tough horn similar to fingernail. It is insensitive and constantly growing. Shoes must be removed and the wall pared into shape approximately every 6 weeks.

SOLE

This protects the underside of the foot. It is, however, quite thin and can easily be punctured by a sharp stone. Inspect the sole regularly to make sure nothing is sticking into it.

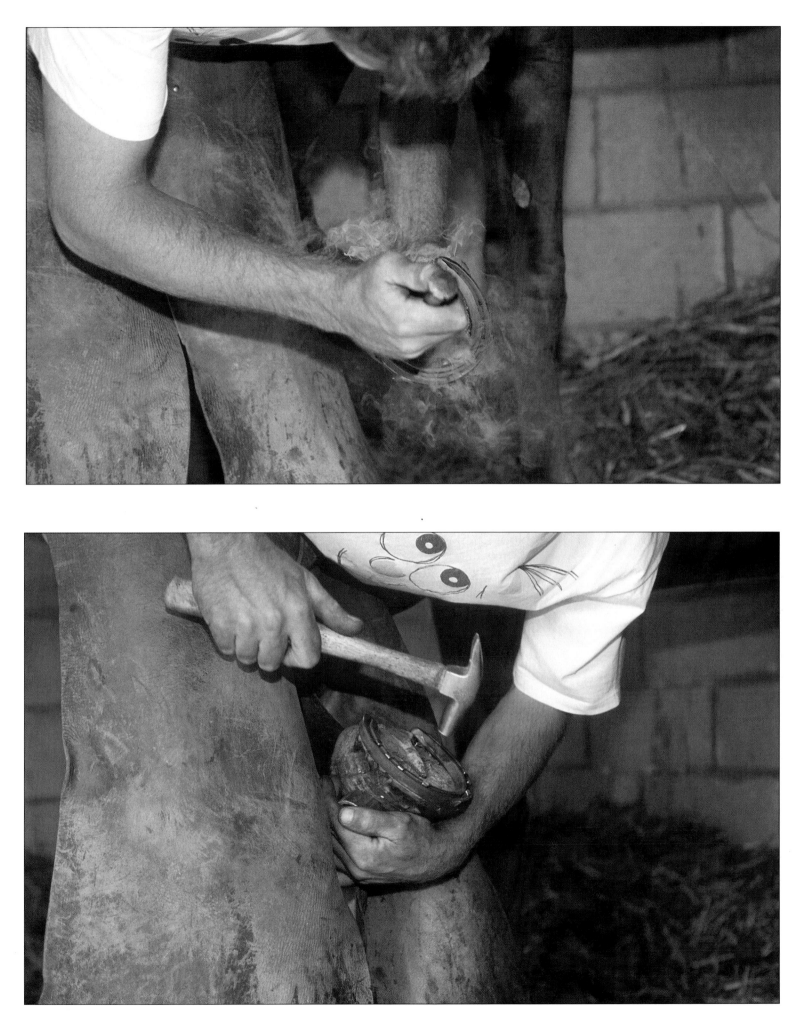

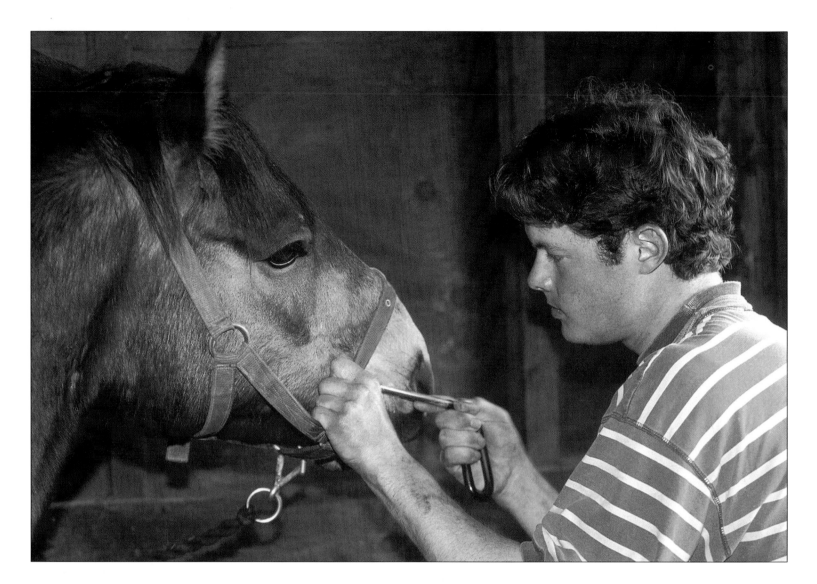

First Aid

Every person owning their own horse should be registered with a veterinary surgeon, preferably one who specializes in horses. Ask an experienced person, such as your instructor or farrier, to recommend a good one. Once you are registered with a veterinary surgery, keep their telephone number to hand in the yard and make sure you pass on this information to anybody involved in looking after your horse. It could well be the very time you are away on holiday that your horse gets ill! Take a good look at your insurance policy. Does it include vets' fees? Remember, a relatively small field injury could incur great cost if your vet is called.

Everybody who has a horse should have a first aid kit and the following are essential components:

Gamgee tissues
Epsom salts
Antiseptic spray and cream
Stockholm tar
Petroleum jelly
Bandages
Gauze or wound dressings
Wound powder
Sponge
Poultice dressings
Rounded scissors
Thermometer

Your first aid kit should prove useful for small cuts and abrasions. Always follow the instructions on the packaging. If you are in doubt about any injury or illness, call your vet immediately. Before you call him, make a note of any symptoms which could help him in his diagnosis and thus save time later on.

Dental Care

Teeth must be checked every six months by the vet. Often, the horse's teeth do not wear uniformly and sharp edges may begin to occur. These edges need to be rasped off by the vet because they will cause great discomfort to the horse, if left, and prevent him from eating properly. If your horse is having trouble eating or seems to be off his food, the problem may well be with his teeth.

ABOVE
All horses should have their teeth checked every six month. This pony is having his teeth rasped by his vet.

RIGHT
A good check over each day will help you to spot any early symptoms of disease or injury ensuring that this horse stays in the best of health at all times.

Chapter Six
Saddlery, and Caring for Your Tack

Saddlery has evolved dramatically over the years, from the highly decorative and heavy leather- and metal-work of the past to the lightweight, hi-tech equipment we see today. Despite its long history, the basic principles of saddlery remain the same as they have always been and early examples of saddles and bridles are still instantly recognizable.

European tack has evolved differently from its American Western counterpart. In Europe, there are two main types of bridle – the ordinary snaffle bridle and the double bridle, which has two bits. There are also different kinds of saddle designed for different types of usage. Most people prefer the general purpose saddle which is designed for all disciplines. Whether you are involved in show jumping, cross-country, or dressage, this saddle is designed to accommodate all.

However, if you are planning to specialize in a certain area, you may wish to buy a more specialized piece of equipment. The dressage saddle is straight cut and allows the rider's leg to fall straighter and longer.

In contrast, the jumping saddle encourages a shorter stirrup length for better balance while jumping.

There are other kinds of saddles for cross-country and racing, but these are still more specialized and are generally not appropriate for day-to-day riding.

FAR LEFT
The snaffle bridle is the most commonly used. This one is combined with a flash noseband and a lightweight plastic bit. However, other varieties of snaffle bits and nosebands can also be used. Always make sure the bridle is correctly fitted. If in doubt, seek expert advice.

LEFT
The general purpose saddle can be used for all disciplines. Whether you are jumping, doing flat work or just hacking around the countryside, this saddle will be suitable. Saddlery should be very well looked after and stitching should be regularly checked and serviced by a qualified saddler. This well fitting, modern saddle, is comfortable for both horse and rider. When buying a new saddle, always consult a qualified saddler to fit the saddle for you.

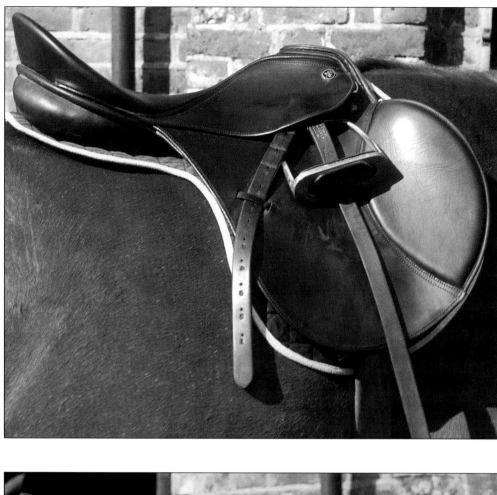

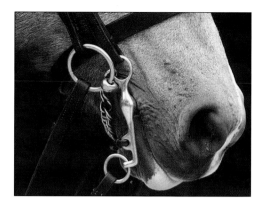

TOP LEFT

The jumping saddle has a forward cut, suitable for a shorter length stirrup. Usually, a general purpose saddle will suffice for most riders, but if you wish to specialize in show jumping, this saddle is a worthwhile investment.

TOP RIGHT

The double bridle is mostly used for dressage and showing. Two bits are used in this bridle, the snaffle and the curb bit. It is essential that the bridle is correctly fitted.

ABOVE

Riding side saddle is becoming more and more popular. The equipment and riding habit are very expensive as they have to be specially made to measure.

LEFT

The dressage saddle is a straight cut saddle used for flat work. It is designed to encourage a deep seat and a long leg which is a characteristic of a good dressage performance.

RIGHT

Western saddlery is beautiful and stylish as well as very practical.

Points of the Bridle

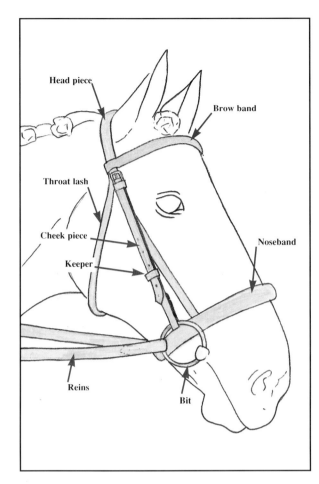

- Head piece
- Brow band
- Throat lash
- Cheek piece
- Keeper
- Noseband
- Reins
- Bit

Points of the Saddle

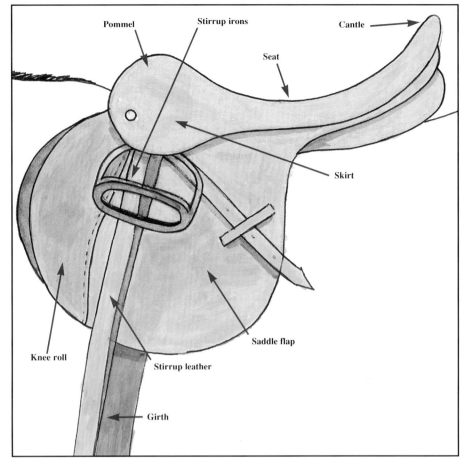

- Pommel
- Stirrup irons
- Cantle
- Seat
- Skirt
- Knee roll
- Saddle flap
- Stirrup leather
- Girth

Western Saddlery

Western bridles have a snaffle or a curb bit, but it is usual for the bits to have long, curved cheek pieces. In general, these bridles are more decorative than their European counterparts and may be plaited or braided. There are two types of Western bridle – the Californian-style and the Texan-style. The Texan bridle has split reins, whereas the Californian has a single length of rein known as a 'romal'.

There are many different designs of Western saddle, but the basic feature is a high horn, high cantle, and a deep, wide seat. Western saddles are intended for long hours out on the range and are therefore well padded for comfort and heavier than the European kind. Most Western saddles are designed with practicality in mind and are sturdy and plain. However, they can also be ornate and highly decorative.

Tack care

All leatherwork should be looked after very carefully and it is recommended that you clean your tack each time you ride.

Cleaning the Bridle: When you clean your tack, carefully check all stitching as old tack with loose or rotten stitching is potentially dangerous. Anything that needs mending should be taken to your local saddler.

First, you should take the bridle apart and lay all the different pieces in front of you. Then you may like to put the bit into soak while you clean the leather.

Thoroughly wash the leather with a wet sponge to remove all the old saddle soap and dirt from the bridle. When you are satisfied that it is perfectly clean, apply saddle soap and gently polish. Rinse the bit and polish it with a clean cloth. Finally, put the bridle back together and hang it up.

Cleaning the Saddle: First, take the girth, numnah, stirrups and leathers from the saddle, then wash the saddle and leathers lightly with a damp sponge to remove all mud and dirt. Rub saddle soap into the leather and polish well. Next, brush off the numnah and girth strap, removing all loose hair and dirt. If the numnah and girth strap are very dirty, they can be washed in soapy water, rinsed and hung out to dry. Remember to wash and dry your stirrup irons and give them a good polish. When everything is clean, put all the pieces back together again.

All saddlery should be stored in a secure, preferably alarmed, cool, dry place. Kept too hot, leather has a tendency to crack – too damp, and the leather will rot. Check the place where you store your tack very carefully.

BELOW
Cleaning your bridle and saddle should be carried out after each time you ride. Your tack will then stay supple and smart and will last for many years. On fine days, the job can be done outside.

RIGHT
This Saddlebred horse looks stunning in his Western-style bridle.

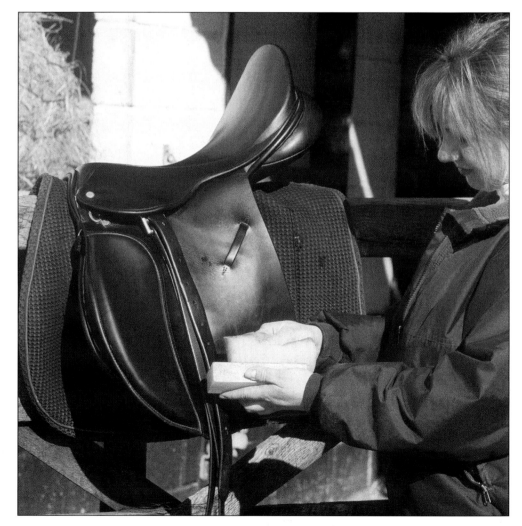

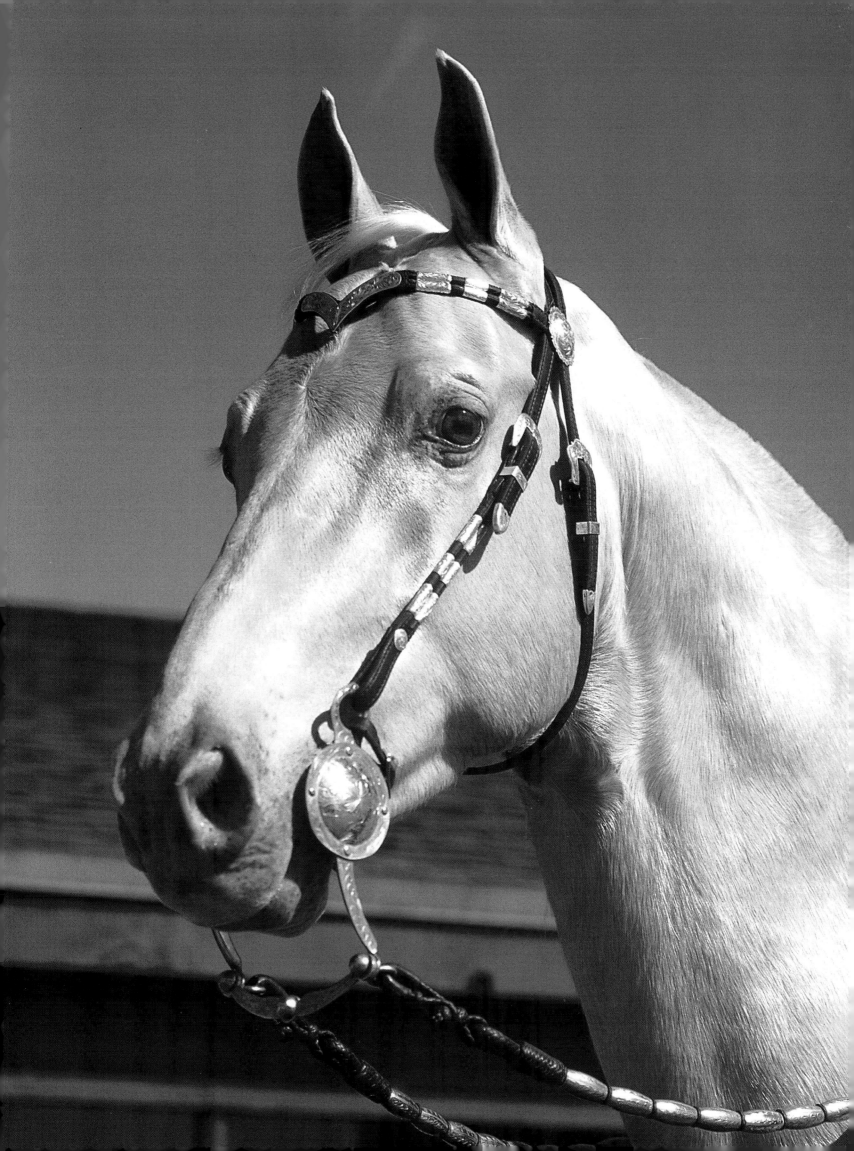

Chapter Seven
Learning to Ride

On the very first occasion, it is better to book yourself a half-hour lesson as a whole hour may be too much for you. A one-to-one lesson with an instructor is the best option and you will find yourself learning a great deal faster than if you are one of a group. Find an approved riding school and it is wise to inspect the facilities and price list before you attend your first lesson.

Mounting

First, make sure the girth strap is tight.
1. Stand on the near side of your pony or horse. Take the reins and your whip in your left hand, keeping the whip on the off side of your pony's neck.
2. Place your left hand about a third of the way up the pony's neck. Then use your right hand to guide your left foot into the stirrup iron, keeping the toes pointed down.

3. When you are ready, jump up using your left foot to propel yourself upwards and swing your right leg clear over the pony's back, taking care to land gently in the saddle. Take up the reins and place your feet in the stirrup irons.

Dismounting

Keeping hold of the reins, take both feet out the stirrup irons, swing your right leg over and land gently.

Mounting

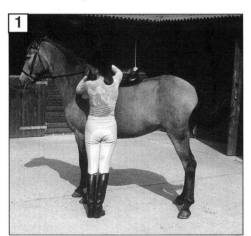

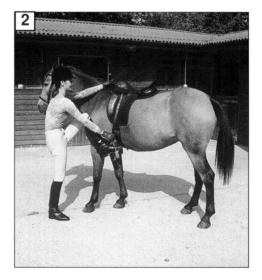

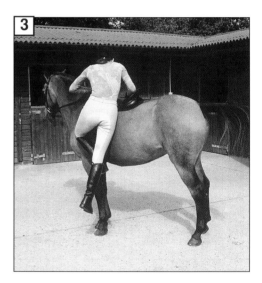

Dismounting

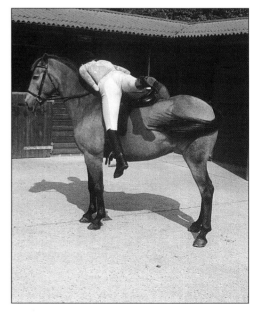

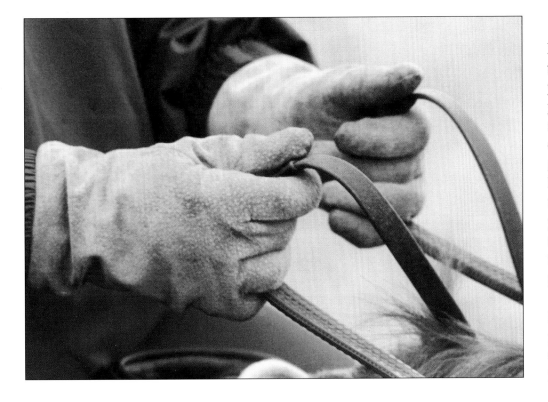

Holding the Reins

Learning to hold the reins correctly will take a lot of practice, particularly when you start trotting. Always remember that your hands should remain as light and as sensitive as possible and that any rapid or over- strong movement may cause great discomfort to your horse. Your hands should go with the movement of the horse at all times. Remember that if you keep your shoulders back and your elbows lightly bent, you should be able to keep your hands in the correct position all the time.

In your initial lessons you will have so many things to think about – position, balance, relaxation and concentration. As your lessons progress, you will begin to feel more at ease

The first time you sit on a horse will seem very strange indeed. You will feel unusually high up and unbalanced. However, as the horse is walked around the school, you will soon start to feel more secure and in harmony with your mount.

Your very first lesson will usually be with an instructor who will hold on to a leading rein while you are getting the feel of the horse and gaining confidence. The first stage is to adopt the correct riding position while the horse is being held still and calm. It is important to get this right as this is the first principle of riding. First, try to sit up as straight as you possibly can with your head up and shoulders back. Try to relax, allowing your legs to hang as long as possible. Hopefully, you will already have the correct length stirrups. Place your feet into them, with the stirrup iron on the ball of your foot and your heels down. Take up the reins in the correct manner (*see above*) keeping your hands about 6 inches apart and just above the horse's withers. Your instructor may allow you to put your hands on the pommel of the saddle for added security while you are led around.

and your instructor will allow you more independence.

Walk

The Walk is a four-time pace characterized by four, clear, even footfalls. Be careful not to push your horse too hard or he may loose his stride. Be very gentle and always try to go with the movement of the horse. Do not over-exaggerate the motion of the walk.

Once you are sufficiently confident on the leading rein, your instructor will put you onto the lunge rein which will allow you greater freedom while allowing him or her to better advise you. Riding on the lunge is an excellent way to learn to ride. It means that the instructor still has the main control over the horse, while you can develop your seat and leg aids and learn to keep your hands and body still.

Trot

The Trot is a two-time pace with each pair of diagonal feet hitting the ground alternately. The trot should be regular and rhythmical. Learning to trot will come as a surprise. You will be amazed to feel how bumpy it is compared to the walk. Your instructor will teach you how to do 'sitting trot' and 'rising trot', both of which need a lot of practice on the lunge before riding alone. The sitting trot is the most difficult and you will need to develop good levels of balance and relaxation. Your body will be absorbing all of the shock and bumps and much practice will be required in order to achieve perfection. The rising trot, however, will be more comfortable for both you and your horse. It will take a little time to master, but after six or seven lessons you should be able to perform it correctly. You must take your weight out of the saddle with every stride, which should be rhythmical and unexaggerated. Your weight should be taken on your knee rather than in your stirrup.

LEFT
This horse is performing a free and regular walk and the rider is giving him freedom of his head so that he can stretch down and relax. This is a good exercise for any horse.

ABOVE
This is a rhythmical and balanced trot and the rider is taking care to sit lightly and still. The use of the dressage saddle will encourage the rider to maintain a deeper seat.

Canter

The Canter is a three-time pace with a clear 'jump' between strides. The canter should not be allowed to become slow or lacking in energy as an incorrect four-time canter may easily develop.

After perfecting the trot, the canter will come easier because, by this stage of your training, your seat and balance will have become better established. The horse will canter with either his right or left leg leading. You will soon be able to distinguish between the two. If you require your horse to canter with the right lead, apply the aids instructing him to canter in a corner of the school on the right rein, he will then naturally strike off with the right lead. If you require a canter with the left lead, apply the aids to make him canter in a suitable corner on the left rein. Most horses and ponies need to come back to trot before changing their canter lead. However, more advanced horses and ponies can be taught to do flying changes where they change their canter lead in a moment of suspension. This is an important skill for dressage horses and show jumpers to learn. It is vital to sit still and relax while cantering trying to keep your shoulders from becoming tense.

Gallop

The Gallop is a four-time pace for open spaces and is the one pace used purely for speed, i.e. in horse racing. All riders long to experience the thrill of a really good gallop in an open space, but only the most experienced riders should try it. If you are lucky enough to have a safe field or an all-weather gallop, make sure your pony is well warmed up before you start off. It is vital to double-check your girth straps before moving off at speed. Use a shorter length of stirrup than usual – this will greatly help your balance. Once you have signalled to your pony to move out of canter and into gallop, incline your body forward, making sure your leg position stays correct with the heel down. Make sure you give yourself plenty of time to slow down.

LEFT
The canter is a three-time pace and should be performed with energy and lightness. Care should be taken to sit up straight and keep your head up. Do not be tempted to lean forward and look down.

BELOW
Going for a gallop is fun and exhilarating for both horse and rider. These horses are being trained for the world of racing.

when asking the horse to further increase speed. If you wish him to slow down his pace, or halt, push him forward, using your legs, so that he can gather himself ready to obey; then resist slightly with your hands, bracing your back and seat muscles to make him slow down.

'Artificial aids' are used when natural aids fail or are not strong enough. Whips, spurs, martingales and other specialized pieces of equipment are all stronger inducements. Initially, they must only be used under experienced instruction. Spurs should only be used by very experienced riders who have great control over their lower legs. Whips can be carried by the less experienced rider, but practice will be needed to keep the whip still and in the correct position.

It takes a great deal of time to master the correct use of each and every aid and novices may tend to over- or under-use them. However, as you gain experience you will begin to realize that they should be used sparingly, with subtlety and refinement, and be completely invisible to the onlooker. When you watch a dressage horse you will notice how he performs a variety of difficult manoeuvres, seemingly without a signal of any kind from his rider.

The Aids

The signals we use to ask the horse to halt, walk, trot, canter, gallop, and even to move sideways, are referred to as 'aids'. 'Natural aids' are signals we transmit to the horse by means of our body movements. Our legs, hands, seat and voice are the main natural aids. We should give these signals gently but firmly; we should never be rough or too abrupt.

When asking the horse to walk forward, we should gently urge him on by bracing our lower leg. At the same time, we should allow our hands forward. The same principle applies

Exercises

'Round the World' (*see opposite*), touching your toes, reaching for your pony's ears – these are great exercises for helping to develop an independent seat and improving balance. At the end of a riding lesson it is always beneficial to spend time on exercises – but make sure you have a good, quiet pony and preferably somebody to hold on to him to prevent him from walking away.

Exercises are great fun and it is a good idea to work towards perfecting them as they are the basis of many pony club competitions. Always hold on tight and wear a body protector for added security.

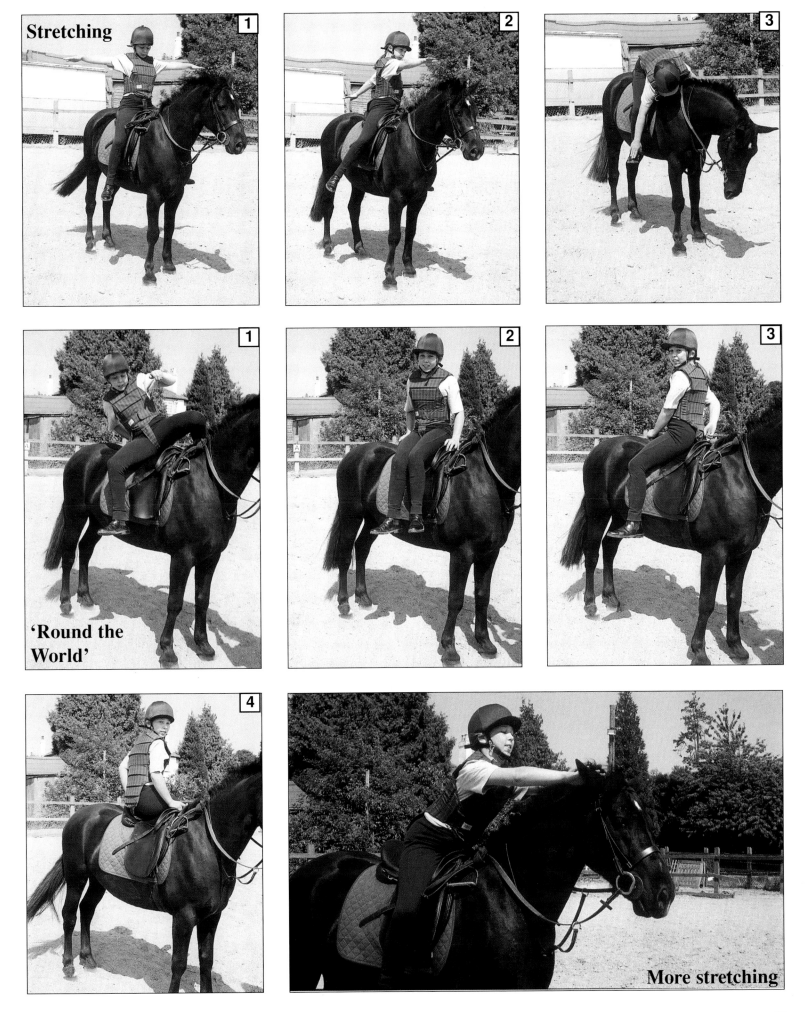

Stretching 1 2 3

'Round the World' 1 2 3

4 **More stretching**

59

Riding Out

Before you attempt to hack out in the countryside you must have mastered all the basics of riding. Hopefully, you will be able to walk, trot, canter and slow down while in the school – all executed with elegance and competence. At this stage it is important for you not to have developed bad habits such as leaning forward or holding your hands too low. There are other common faults but regular instruction will help prevent these from developing. Although you now have confidence in your own abilities, you must feel the same way about your mount before venturing out. Make sure he has a reputation for good behaviour when out on a hack.

Safety

Once you feel perfectly confident, you can start to hack out. Your riding school is sure to arrange hacks and will be happy for you to join in once they feel confident of your riding ability. At first, avoid busy roads which are likely to make you feel nervous. Only experienced riders, capable of maintaining the strictest control, should ride in traffic. Whether hacking out on major or minor roads, always wear bright fluorescent clothing. This will allow motorists to see you from a good distance and give them time to slow down. Always remember to thank motorists who do slow down for you.

When hacking out on roads, always think ahead. Be prepared for the unexpected. Horses are naturally wary animals and, surprised by something unexpected, such as a flapping piece of plastic or a discarded bag of rubbish, may suddenly shy away, swerving into oncoming traffic. Put a quiet horse in the lead, the others following behind, and take extra care. On the first few occasions you venture out, it may also be necessary to avoid open fields or areas where your horse usually gallops or canters as this will cause him to become overexcited when he hits the open area! The ideal spot, while you are still building up your confidence, is a

place where there are tracks and bridle-paths where you can walk, trot and canter in safety. Remember, when riding out, to take a hoof pick with you – an essential tool should your horse get a stone in his foot. Always remember to tell your stable yard where you are going and take some money or a card for the telephone with you.

The more experience you gain, the more you will enjoy riding out and your horse will enjoy it as much as you do. As an added bonus, the view of the countryside is even better from the back of a horse because you are much higher up than you would be if simply on foot.

Riding Away from Home

There are many different types of riding holiday from which to choose and you can either take your own horse with you or hire one from the holiday centre. Riding holidays can be taken abroad or at home and will widen the scope of your riding experience to take in beach, mountain, desert and forest. Whatever you choose, you will have a great time!

This is a good opportunity to meet like-minded friends, and will help consolidate your relationship with your pony. On long hacks, far from home, you will become more interdependent for you will be trekking with him over largely unknown territory under very different conditions. This will lead you to a pay more attention to your pony's needs and develop a new kind of independence. Some holiday riding centres provide instruction courses where you can learn show jumping or dressage or ride cross-country and you will find the experience so rewarding that you will wish to repeat it again and again.

The correct equipment is essential and the centre will most likely supply you with a list in advance; but bad weather gear, several pairs of jodhpurs, sun cream, first aid kit, T shirts, boots and safety gear are just some of the more important requirements.

LEFT
Hacking out on roads and tracks is quite an adventure; but always remember to take extra care in traffic. Always give clear hand signals and don't forget to thank drivers who slow down for you.

ABOVE
It is the dream of most riders to be able to go for a gallop on the beach. This happy holidaymaker will now have an experience to remember.

Chapter Eight
How to Lunge

Lunging is a great way of exercising horses. It helps to develop your horse's physique and gives you a chance to examine his way of going. You will also find that he greatly enjoys the experience. To lunge your horse you will need a bridle without reins and a noseband, a lunging cavesson, a lunge rein and a lunge whip and side-reins. A full set of brushing boots is an essential piece of equipment because to lunge on a circle is hard work and the horse could accidentally brush or kick himself if not properly protected.

Make sure you are wearing gloves and a riding hat, even though you are not mounted. It is best to lunge in a fairly confined area to prevent your pony from becoming too excited. When lunging, stand on the spot in the centre of the area, pivoting round as the horse moves around you in a circle. Hold the lunge rein in one hand, letting it out gently, and your whip in the other to guide your pony out and away from you. The lunge rein, whip and horse's outline should form the shape of a triangle. Be careful not to let the rein drag on the ground and refrain from making jerky or sudden movements with the whip. The whip must be used for gentle encouragement only, not to hit the horse in order to urge him forward. You must not allow the horse to lose his trust in you.

When lunging, commands are given by voice rather that touch. If your pony has been lunged before, he will already know what *whoa, walk, trot* and *canter* means. If he is less experienced, he will come to learn the commands through repetition and gentle encouragement with the lunge whip.

Lunge your horse for ten to fifteen minutes each way. Side-reins should be used to steady him and will encourage him to work in a better outline. Start off with the side-reins quite loose to allow time for your horse to adjust to them. They can then be shortened over a period of time, but do not over-tighten them or you will restrict his natural pace. Refrain from leading

your horse with side-reins attached.

When your horse has become well accustomed to lunging with no one on his back, it is a good idea for your instructor to give you the occasional lesson when you can ride him on the lunge yourself. There are many individual exercises which can be performed on the lunge, in walk, trot and even canter. Touching your toes, head, knees and putting your hands out to the sides will help improve your balance. As you become more confident, you will find that you can ride for short periods without stirrups. To quit your

stirrups, it is best to cross them over in front of the saddle or, if they are in your way, and you plan to ride without stirrups for a long time, you may wish to remove them completely.

Lessons on the lunge, while mounted, and being able to lunge successfully are both important skills to develop. There are times when it may not be possible to ride a horse due to injury in the saddle area or because he has been lame. This is where lunging is invaluable for he can be gently schooled and exercised in this way until he is fully recovered.

ABOVE
A mounted lesson in lunging will help build a beginner's confidence, for the instructor retains full control of the horse during the entire procedure.

Chapter Nine
Working Towards Competition

Dressage

When you are confident that your riding ability has reached a good average standard, you can choose to concentrate on one of the different aspects of equestrianism. Dressage is a discipline arising from the classical tradition which involves training the horse to a very high standard of athleticism and control. There are no quick routes to training for dressage and most of the work is carried out in the school. The performance of dressage consists of walk, trot and canter and the paces are improved and perfected through training. Specific movements must be performed in each pace. The quality of dressage is judged on the horse rather than the rider, which means that a fair-

ly inexperienced rider can be quite successful provided he or she has a very well trained horse.

The horse is examined by means of a dressage test which is a set sequence of movements performed in various paces. Each movement is given a mark. The judges will be looking for obedience, suppleness, good paces and an improved natural outline. It is advisable to use a special dressage saddle which is straight cut and allows for a greater length of leg against the horse's side. A snaffle bridle is worn for the earlier levels of competition progressing to a double bridle when advanced levels are reached.

Tests are carried out in a dressage arena, the rider being obliged to follow specific markers. *(See below).*

RIGHT
Riding a dressage test requires good powers of memory and concentration as well as lots of practice. This rider is performing her test in the dressage section of a one-day-event. Her pony is not only required to perform his test with obedience and elegance but will later be expected to show jump and gallop cross-country.

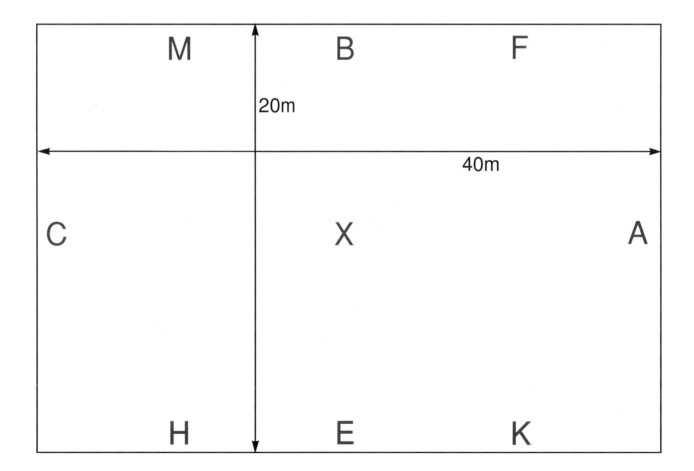

Show Jumping

Should you decide to jump your pony, it would be wise to incorporate dressage training with your jumping practice. All professional show jumpers are trained in flat work and it is essential to their overall training. Even if you particularly enjoy jumping, it is not a good idea to overdo it. Once a week is quite sufficient; otherwise your pony will become thoroughly bored rather than fresh and interested when practice jumping begins. It is usual to start his training with trotting poles. This will encourage him to think about obstacles, widen his confidence and make him more athletic. Trotting poles are always good to start with and will help the rider develop his own jumping ability. At this stage it is a good idea to practise your own jumping position. Your stirrups should be about 2 holes shorter than for ordinary riding. Keep your body

LEFT AND BELOW
Successful show jumping requires plenty of ability in both horse and rider.

inclined forward and your leg and thigh position as normal. As you go over the jump your hands should be allowed forward as your body folds forward. Practise this while trotting or cantering around the school or field.

Next we proceed to the use of cavaletti, small jumps which can be interspersed between trotting poles. It is very important to get the spacing exactly right between each jump and pole – your instructor will be able to help you here. The jumps should be kept small as the object of the exercise is not to jump as high as possible but to encourage athleticism and confidence.

Moving on to small courses built in the school or in the field, keep the jumps small to encourage confidence in both pony and rider. Make the jumps interesting. Brightly painted fillers and poles will introduce your pony to proper show jumping conditions so that when you take him to his first competition he will have fewer

shocks to contend with. If you are intending to compete, make sure you can jump slightly higher jumps at home than you are likely to encounter in competition. Most horses will always go better on their home ground so you must be fully prepared when travelling to a strange venue.

BELOW
Trotting poles are an ideal way to encourage inexperienced riders and horses to show jump. Your instructor will help you make certain the poles are correctly placed.

RIGHT
As confidence grows, small combinations can be put up to take the learning process a stage further.

Eventing

Eventing combines the three disciplines of dressage, show jumping and cross-country and is a real test of both horse and rider. Usually, it is a one-day-event but at higher levels the competition is held over three days.

At a one-day-event, the riders will all be expected to perform the same dressage test, which must be ridden from memory. This in itself is a hard task as you will have so many other things to think about. The dressage test must be performed with your horse wearing a simple snaffle bridle and saddle. Martingales and other more complicated pieces of tack are definitely forbidden, neither will your horse be allowed to wear any brushing or over-reach boots.

Your dressage test will be carefully marked by the judges and the score you receive will affect your total mark at the end of the day.

Next, you will be required to negotiate a set of jumps. The aim is of course to jump clear. Again, this will affect your final marking and position in the competition.

Next comes the cross-country phase. Cross-country jumps are substantial and solid and are laid out at intervals around the course for you to jump. Make sure you walk the course thoroughly beforehand to familiarize yourself with the lie of the land; the last thing you want is to lose your way! The aim is to jump clear in an optimum time which will be set by the judges.

At the end of the competition, any penalties you have incurred will be added up and the winner announced.

LEFT AND THIS PAGE
The three phases of eventing are dressage,
show jumping and cross-country. All are of
equal difficulty and a real test of both horse
and rider.

Chapter Ten
Preparation for Competition

Now that you are fully accustomed to riding and caring for your horse or pony, you can look forward to attending your first gymkhana or horse show. You will be surprised to find how many different classes there are to choose from and at the larger shows, the number of classes are daunting to say the least.

Before you decide which show appeals to you most, you must think about transport. If the ground is within hacking distance, there is no problem. Further afield, and you will need some means of transporting your horse, either by box or trailer. If you own your own transport, again, no problem; if you do not, it will be necessary to hire or borrow a suitable vehicle. Organize this well before the show to avoid disappointment when you later find there is nobody available to transport your pony to the show ground.

Once your transport is booked, it is time to decide the events in which you will be competing and to fill in the entry form. This should be completed very carefully to avoid the costly mistake of entering the wrong class when your money will probably not be refundable. Make sure you send in your payment and entry form well before the due date to ensure everything arrives in good time.

The day before the show is a good time to give your pony a very thorough grooming and to wash his tail and mane. If the weather is cold, it is not recommended that you wash him completely but it is fine to do so if it is hot – he will most likely enjoy it, too! It is best to keep the pony in his stable the night before the show when it is a good idea to put a clean rug on him to keep him as clean as possible after all your good work.

There are many things you will also need to do. Make sure your clothes are clean and well pressed. Check over your show jacket, jodhpurs, tie, shirt, gloves, boots and hair ribbons. They should all be spotless. If you decide to wear a tie pin, make sure it is to hand. Once you are satisfied that everything is in order you should check that all your pony's gear is immaculate. Clean and check all the tack he will be wearing. If he wears any kind of boots, make sure they are clean, in fact, all your pony's travelling gear should be clean and in good repair.

Once you know you are as well prepared as you can possibly be, your confidence and excitement will grow and you can really start looking forward to the show.

On the morning of the great event you will rise very early. Make sure you have everything you need – all loaded up and ready to go. Do not change into your clean show outfit until the very last minute. You still have plenty of work to do.

Take your pony from his stable. You will need to give him another grooming to remove any marks from his coat. Once he has been thoroughly groomed, plait his mane and tail and get him ready to travel.

Hoof Care

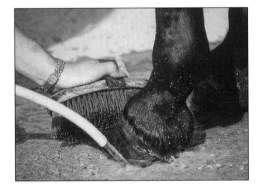

Hooves must be scrubbed, dried and oiled in preparation for the competition.

Trimming Face and Ears

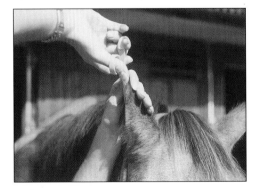

Trim excess hair from the ears and chin. Take special care, however, that you don't cut your horse, or accidentally stab him with the end of the scissors. Get an experienced person to help you trim the ears.

Trimming Legs

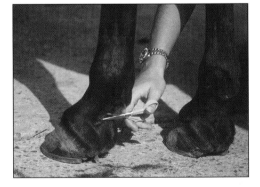

Trimming the hair from the legs makes a cobby horse look finer. It is also important for showing the horse's legs off to their best advantage.

Plaiting the Mane

1

Thoroughly comb the mane and divide it up into an odd number of sections, i.e. 5 or 7. With the forelock, this makes up an even number which is supposed to be lucky. Separate each section with elastic bands.

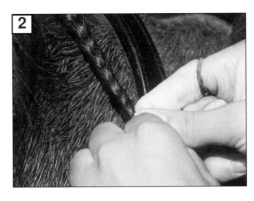

2

Take the first section and plait it right to the very end.

3

Using a needle and strong plaiting thread, secure the end. Select a thread which matches the colour of your horse's mane, black for a bay, brown for a chestnut.

4

Turn the end of the plait under and sew in to neaten the edges.

5

Roll the plait under until it forms a small neat bobble. Make sure that it is nice and tight. When you get to the end, sew it all together trying not to show too much thread.

6

Finally, trim the excess thread off carefully.

Plaiting the Tail

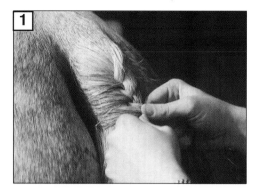

1

After thoroughly brushing and combing the tail, begin to incorporate small sections of tail hair starting at the top next to the dock. Take in small sections from either side forming a neat shape as you go.

2

Continue down the tail, making sure the plait stays neat and even.

3

When you reach the end of the dock, carry on plaiting the top section only until you reach the end.

4

Turn the plait under and sew in to hide the end.

THESE PAGES
Tail plaiting is a way of showing off the horse's hindquarters as well as giving the tail an attractive, well-groomed appearance. Getting the plait perfect takes time and practice, but the end result is definitely well worthwhile.

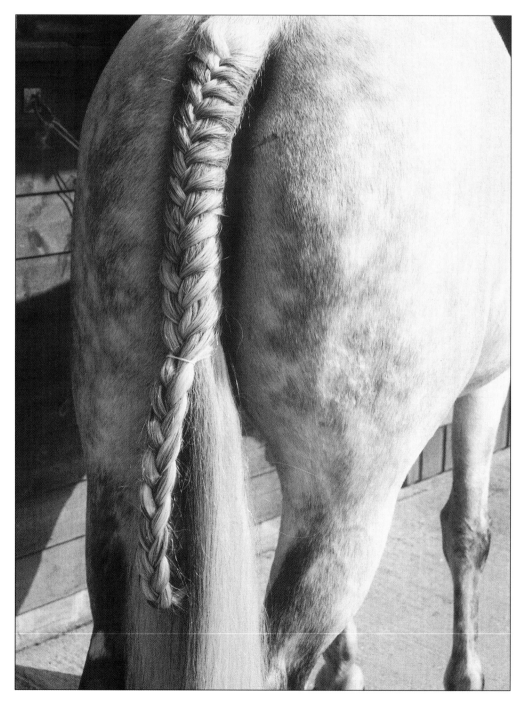

Travelling

Before transporting your horse any-where, it is most important that he is adequately protected. Most important are his tail and legs. These should be protected with bandages or wraps. There are many kinds from which to choose.

Putting on a Tail Bandage

First roll up the tail bandage, starting at the tag end. Firmly wind on the bandage, starting at the top end of the tail.

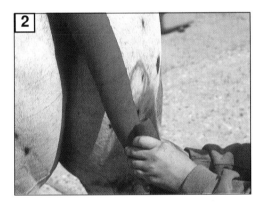

Wind the tail bandage right to the end of the dock.

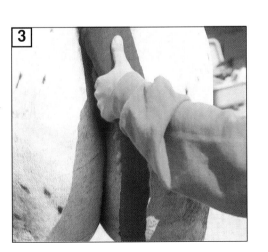

Tie the tag end with a bow, then tuck the tail between the horse's legs.

Travelling Equipment

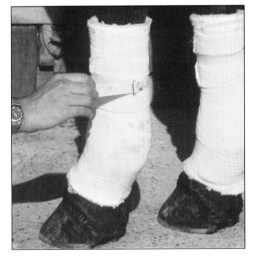

It is important to protect your horse's legs while travelling. Wrap soft gamgee around the legs and secure it with leg bandages.

Protect the knees with knee boots.

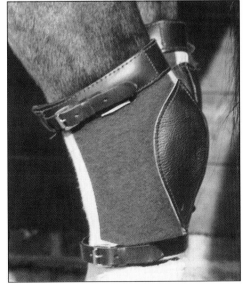

It is important that the hock is protected. These hock boots are ideal.

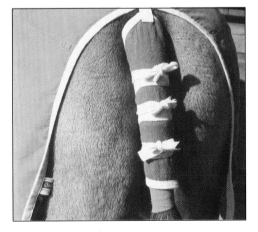

Tail guards are useful for holding the tail bandage in position and offer extra protection. Finally, it is a good idea to put a light rug on in summer and a heavier one in winter in order to protect your horse's coat and keep it clean.

Clothing for the Show

When attending a show you must look just as well turned out as your horse. Show clothing is very expensive, but it is possible to buy some items second hand. A tweed hacking jacket and light coloured jodhpurs with jodhpur boots will suffice. However, as you progress, you may wish to invest in a black jacket and long boots. Of course, the obligatory velvet riding hat is essential.

For riding cross country, a coloured sweat shirt and matching skull cap is required and, most importantly, a body protector. A body protector should also be used under a show jacket when jumping and may even be worn for hacking out in the countryside.

If you plan to show your pony in a ridden or in hand class, the dress requirements are very strict indeed and if you turn up with the wrong equipment you may be heavily penalized. For instance, if your choice of class is working a hunter pony, your dress will be very different than if you choose to enter the riding pony class.

LEFT
This rider is well turned out for a riding pony class.

ABOVE
Dress for the working hunter class is illustrated here. The dress is more subdued than that of the riding pony class.

Chapter Eleven
Breeds of the World

An equine 'breed' is defined as a group of horses or ponies that have been selectively bred to produce consistent characteristics of height, colour, conformation and action. If a horse is 'pure-bred' it means that both its parents will be recognized by a particular breed society. Horses who display particular characteristics, but are not 'pure-bred' are known as 'types'. A Hunter-type is a good example and the American Pinto is a 'colour-type' rather than a true breed.

Today, there are many different breeds in the world and their number, comformation and colour are constantly changing: this is due to the environment and refinement of particular breeds by man. Many breeds, particularly heavy horses, have virtually died out altogether simply because they are no longer required in today's society. However, with growing interest in showing, some heavy breeds have been revived and are thriving in smaller numbers.

The decline of the heavier horse has been compensated by the increase in popularity of the riding horse with many new stud books being opened up throughout the world. These are divided into two types 'open', which means that the mare and stallion do not have to be of the same breed but do have to be of pedigree stock, and 'closed', which means that both parents must be of the same breed and registered pedigree stock.

Most breeds fall into definite classes, hotblood, warmblood, coldblood and pony. The hotbloods are pure-bred, highly strung, pedigree horses such as the Thoroughbred and Arab. Warmbloods are slightly heavier, stronger animals, commonly used as riding horses and particularly used for dressage. Their strength comes from their ancestry from heavy horses which are classified as coldblooded. Ponies are the native breeds of the world, for example, the Dartmoor. All ponies fall under the height of 14.2hh.

However, some horses slip through this system, for example, the hunter, hack and cob which are not registered in the stud books along with the Australian Brumby which is not a recognized breed.

Horses have evolved all over the world, the most famous being the Arab. It is hard to pinpoint its exact origins but it is generally thought to have run wild in the Yemen in the Arabian peninsula. These horses proved to be extremely swift and tough with excellent stamina. It is for this reason that the racing Thoroughbred was bred from three Arab stallions, the *Byerly Turk*, the *Darley Arabian* and the *Godolphin Arabian.*

In Australia, imported horses escaped from the first British settlers in 1790 to become the feral Brumby. The first recognized breed to come from Australia was known as the Waler because it originated in New South Wales. It was formed by crossing Arab, Thoroughbred and Anglo-Arab stallions with local cobby mares. It was later renamed the Australian Stock Horse.

Asia is the home of many of the more exotic breeds, including the Indian Manipur (a type) which was the first polo pony.

The oldest living breed of horse still survives in China. The Mongolian Wild Horse was discovered by Colonel Przewalski in 1881.

Most of today's popular riding horses come from Europe. The most illustrious being the Lipizzaner, the white stallion from Lipizza near Trieste. These are the famous mounts of the Spanish Riding School in Vienna.

With the increasing popularity of dressage, many people are choosing German and Dutch breeds. For example, the Hanoverian, Holstein and Trakehner from West Germany, the Dutch Warmblood from Holland and the warmbloods from Belgium and Sweden make excellent dressage horses. They have excellent paces, great intelligence and the natural aptitude to learn the difficult movements required at the top levels of the sport.

Horses in America died out at the end of the ice Age. They were reintroduced in 1511 when the Spanish arrived. Many of these escaped and bred in the wild, becoming known as Mustangs; these were used by the Native Americans. The tribe Nez Perce later bred the first recognized Indian breed, the 'Appaloosa'.

Later, as the colonists came, bringing their own horses with them, new breeds started to emerge. Among the earliest was the Morgan and the Narrangansett Pacer, which was followed by the Quarter Horse, the oldest surviving American breed: the name originates from the Virginians who bred it and raced it over a quarter of a mile. It proved extremely strong and agile and was used as a cow pony and at rodeos.

Other horses, such as the Palamino and Pinto, though not strictly breeds but colour types are, however, recognized as breeds in the United States.

Canada has no true breeds of its own: the Canadian Cutting Horses is defined as a type.

American Saddle Horse

Andalusian

Appaloosa

Ardennes

Brabant

Camargue

Cleveland Bay

Dutch Warmblood

Falabella

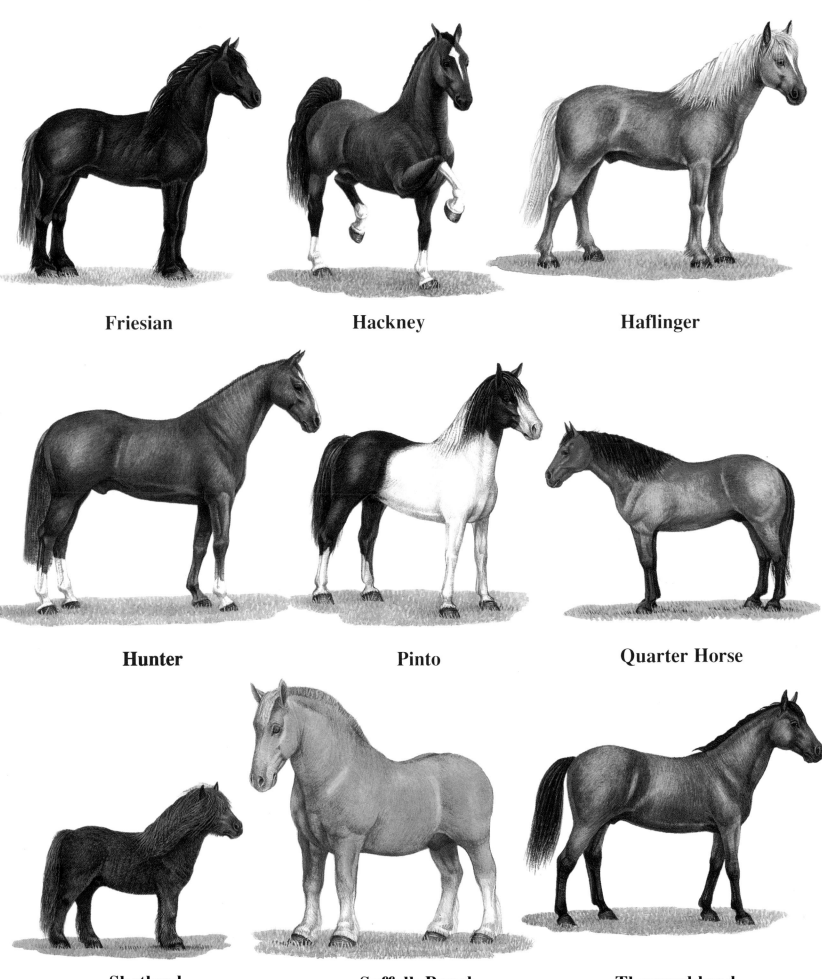

Friesian

Hackney

Haflinger

Hunter

Pinto

Quarter Horse

Shetland

Suffolk Punch

Thoroughbred

Glossary

Aids Recognized signals used by the rider to pass instructions to the horse. *Natural aids* are conveyed through the legs, hands, body and voice and *artificial aids* include whips, spurs and other items such as martingales.

At Grass A horse who either lives in a field all year round or who is turned out from time to time.

Bit The mouthpiece fitted to the bridle used to aid the rider's control of the horse. There are many different kinds such as the snaffle.

Box, to To lead a horse up the ramp and into a horse box or trailer.

Brushing When the inside of a horse's hind or foreleg is struck with the opposite leg. Brushing boots can be used as a protection against this.

Cantle Extreme back ridge of a saddle.

Cavalletti Small jumps used to school horses and riders.

Cavesson Either a simple noseband or a *lunging cavesson* used for breaking and schooling horses on the lunge rein.

Chaff Finely chopped hay used to add bulk to the feed or to prevent the horse from bolting his food.

Cob A horse of medium size, larger than a pony, and characterized by its stocky, powerful build.

Concussion Continuous banging of the horse's feet on hard ground. May cause swelling and lameness.

Diagonals At the trot pace, the rider can either ride on the left or the right diagonal. During rising trot, the rider can either rise when the horse's right foreleg hits the ground (right diagonal) or he can rise when the horse's left foreleg hits the ground (left diagonal).

Double Bridle Through the use of a bridle with two bits, the snaffle and the curb, the rider can exercise a greater degree of control over his mount than he could with an ordinary bridle.

Dressage The training of the horse to perform in the classical tradition. The aim is to achieve obedience, control and suppleness.

Eventing A competition involving the three disciplines of dressage, cross-country and show jumping.

Farrier A skilled craftsman who specializes in shoeing and caring for a horse's feet.

Frog The V-shaped part of the horse's foot which acts as a shock absorber.

Gamgee Gauze covered cotton wool used in bandages or to give extra support or protection to a horse's legs.

Grooming The daily routine of cleaning, brushing and keeping the horse's coat, mane and tail free from grease and dirt.

Grooming Kit The tools used for grooming – combs, brushes, etc..

Hack A term used for going out for a ride. Can also be used to describe a type of horse.

Hand A unit of 10 cm (4 inches) used to measure the height of a horse.

Hay net A loosely woven rope bag made to contain hay.

Hoof Pick A metal implement used for removing mud and stones from a horse's hooves.

Hunter A type of horse of any breed suitable to be ridden to hounds.

Irons Stirrup irons are attached to the saddle and are designed to support the rider's feet.

Leading Rein Long rope attached to the bit by which the horse can be led.

Livery Stables A place where an owner can keep his horse and for which a fee is charged.

Lunge Training a horse on a long rein attached to a cavesson when the trainer uses a lunge whip to encourage the horse.

Manege An arena or school which has been marked out in the traditional method. Used for schooling horses and for teaching people to ride.

Martingale An item of tack used to give the rider a greater degree of control over a horse.

Mucking Out The process of cleaning out a horse's stable.

Nearside The left-hand side of a horse.

Offside The right-hand side of a horse.

Palamino A horse with a coat of various shades of gold and a white mane and tail.

Points of the horse Terms and names given to the various parts of the horse's body.

Pommel The centre front of the astride saddle.

Pony A small horse standing at 14.2 hands high or less.

Pull, to (mane and tail) The process of tidying and thinning the mane or tail.

Rising Trot The trot pace performed with the rider rising up out of the saddle with each stride of the horse.

Saddle Horse A horse suitable for riding.

Saddle Soap A preparation for cleaning and preserving leather.

School An area marked out in a traditional way where horses are trained and exercised.

Shoe, to The procedure of fitting and securing metal shoes onto a horse's feet.

Side Reins Reins used to steady the horse and improve his outline. One end of the rein is fixed to the bit and the other to either the front of the saddle or a roller.

Snaffle Bit A type of simple mouthpiece of which there are many different kinds.

Spurs An artificial aid or device fitted to the rider's boot to enourage the horse forward.

Surcingle A strap, usually of webbing, which passes over the horse's back and under his belly and is used to secure a rug or saddle.

Tack A general term used for describing items of saddlery.

Thoroughbred Dating from the 17th century, this is probably one of the most famous breeds of horse.

Trailer A form of transportation for horses which is towed behind another vehicle.

Turn Out To put a horse out in the field.

Vice Any bad habit a horse may develop.

Wisp A woven and twisted clump of hay used to massage a horse's skin.